Essential Elements of

Human Resource Management

Sally Howe

Sally Howe is a senior lecturer in the Business School of the University of the
West of England, Bristol.

Series adviser: Bob Cudmore BEd, MBA, Head of Management and Professional
Studies Division, South Birmingham College

Technical adviser: Jenny Rankin BA (Hons), MSc, MIPD, MCIM, South Birmingham
College

Published in association with South Birmingham College
DP Publications Ltd
1995

A CIP catalogue reference for this book is available from the British Library

ISBN 1 85805 145 2

Typeset by Nigel Jordan, Jordan Publishing Design

Printed in Great Britain by the Guernsey Press Co. Ltd, Vale, Guernsey

ii

Preface

Aim of the book

The aim of this book is to provide the Essential Elements of Human Resource Management at a price which students can afford. It can be used as a course text, supplemented by lectures, introductory reading or revision on a variety of management and business courses, such as the BTEC Higher National Diploma/Certificate in Business Studies, Certificate in Management, Certificate in Business Administration, Certificate in Marketing, Certificate in Personnel Management, etc. The text has also been written to link with the National Vocational Qualification (NVQ) Occupational Standards for Managers covering the elements in the Managing People area. The text would be helpful for those studying at NVQ levels 3,4 and 5.

Key features

Essential Elements of Human Resource Management is a workbook which is divided into eight chapters and arranged in a logical teaching sequence. Activities, which aim to promote understanding of the principles, are set at frequent intervals. These form an integral part of the text and the solutions add to the student's knowledge and ability to apply what they are reading.

At the end of each chapter there are references to further reading and other library resources (where appropriate), as well as a variety of exercises. Some are intended for self-assessment by the student and answers are provided at the back of the book. Others are suitable for setting by the lecturer and answers or marking guides are provided in the Lecturer's Supplement. These include multiple choice questions, which test specific knowledge and allow rapid marking, practice questions for advanced students, and assignments.

Lecturer's supplement

The Lecturer's Supplement is available free of charge to lecturers adopting the book as a course text. It provides answers or guides to help with student assessment.

How to use the series

The Essential Elements series provides coverage of the main subject areas of business studies so that students can pick and mix titles to suit the requirements of their own particular courses. All the books in the series are intended to be used as workbooks, since students learn best by being pro-active. Each book covers the essential elements of the subject, so that the core of any course at that level is covered, leaving the lecturer to add supplementary material if required. Approximately 70 hours of study material is provided.

Other titles in the series include Business Economics, Marketing, Financial Accounting, Management Accounting, Business Information Systems, Business Statistics and Quantitative Methods.

Contents

1 An introduction to Human Resource Management

1.1 Introduction

This chapter explains the term human resource management and outlines the evolution of the ideas and techniques associated with it. It looks at human resource management roles and discusses how policies are determined. The relationship between human resource management within an organisation and the external environment is also investigated. Finally, the issue of human resource management as a professional activity will be debated.

On completing this chapter you should be able to:

☐ discuss what is meant by human resource management;

☐ describe the main human resource management roles and policy areas;

☐ identify the main external factors which impact upon organisational HRM;

☐ evaluate human resource management as a profession.

1.2 What is human resource management?

One of the difficulties associated with the study of human resource management (HRM) is the broad range of ideas and techniques encompassed within it, which has resulted in a failure to provide one common interpretation of this study area.

In the literature the terms welfare, personnel management, industrial relations and employee relations have all been used to describe activities in this field of study. More recently the term human resource management has become more frequent, replacing in many organisations the more traditional personnel management label. The question is, are all these terms interchangeable or are there subtle differences of content that should be attributed to each one?

In answering this question, one approach that can be taken is to trace back the various terms to their point of origin to see if a historical perspective helps to clarify their meanings. The various traditions are outlined below:

1. The welfare tradition

    The earliest traditions of what is now called HRM came from the welfare role introduced in the early 20th century. At this time, before the advent of the welfare state, many employees suffered greatly if they were unable to work, and general health and safety standards were much lower than those of today. In the early part of the century some employers made determined efforts to improve the nutrition and welfare of their employees, sometimes creating housing and recreation facilities around the working areas. Developing out of this trend, several organisations appointed welfare officers to take responsibility for maintaining good working conditions for the staff. The welfare role in the U.K. today has largely been adopted by the state but the heritage of concern for health and safety is still present in the HRM function.

2. The employment management tradition

Another developing trend in the early part of the century was the desire to improve work methods by studying the most efficient ways to organise labour. Researchers attempted to introduce "scientific management" systems which made better use of working time. This scientific management tradition created an interest in job definition, job design, workflow study and recruitment, selection and training techniques. The ability to quantify and measure work and provide effective guidelines for recruitment and training expanded the role of the welfare officers, so the title personnel manager began to replace it. Personnel managers, were still closely allied to the workforce and the welfare role, but in addition they had a responsibility to the management of the organisation to utilise labour effectively. This led to the role of personnel being seen as one which mediated between managers and the workforce in general.

3. The industrial relations tradition

This view was also enhanced by the role personnel managers adopted in the relationship between trade unions and management. Throughout the century membership of trade unions expanded, reaching a peak in the late 1970's. With this increased focus on trade unions, negotiation and collective bargaining dominated the work of many personnel managers of the time, eventually causing a new title to be coined, that of industrial relations manager. Industrial relations tends to be associated with unionised activities, but can also describe more general activities associated with the management of groups of employees. As the status and number of trade union members declined in the 1980's and 90's, and more organisations existed without unions at all, the term employee relations began to replace the more traditional industrial relations title. Various writers have argued that industrial relations is about the management of groups of employees and their collective rights, whereas employee relations is more concerned with matters relating to the individual. In practice, however, these areas overlap to a large extent.

4. The specialist advisor tradition

Other roles associated with HRM developed to fill the need to provide specialist advice to managers. Employment law has become more complex over time, with both U.K. and E.U. requirements to comply with. Legal experts are often part of the HRM department. Specialists are also needed for the increasingly sophisticated range of selection devices introduced in recent years. Statistical analysts may help with future planning for employees using a wide range of computer techniques. Training and management development programmes also require in-depth knowledge of particular subjects. All these areas have their own job titles and responsibilities, and many of these functions are fulfilled by independent consultants rather than full-time employees of the organisation.

Bringing together these various strands, today the term human resource management is used widely to incorporate all the activities outlined above. As such it is an umbrella term for a varied and specialist range of tasks associated with people management.

Activity

From the following list of activities decide what tradition(s) they developed from:
- ☐ Health and Safety
- ☐ Stress counselling
- ☐ Selection interviewing
- ☐ Induction training
- ☐ Redundancy selection
- ☐ Wage negotiation
- ☐ Monitoring equal opportunities

Although arguments can be put forward to propose various other origins for each technique, generally stress counselling and health and safety can be said to follow on from the welfare tradition. Health and safety also have a specialist legal component together with equal opportunities monitoring and redundancy selection. More general employment management activities are the selection interviewing and induction training of employees, and industrial relations concerns are evident in wage negotiation and redundancy selection.

For other commentators the term Human Resource Management has a much more specific meaning. Techniques of HRM evolved during the 1980's and 1990's as a management response to the changes caused by the factors outlined below:

1. Economic pressures

   The economic recession of the early 1980's led to pressure on many organisations to become more efficient, flexible and productive. The traditional style of personnel management was seen as too rigid and bureaucratic, and the industrial relations systems were felt to encourage conflict in the workplace.

2. Political pressures

   Politically, the Conservative government was elected with a mandate to reduce the power of trade unions and restore management's right to manage. The old consensus collective bargaining arrangements were felt to restrict the necessary changes in production, and many other personnel systems were criticised for rigidity.

3. Structural change

   Structurally, the U.K. economy, together with that of many other countries, saw a decline in employment in manufacturing and an increase in the service sector. Information Technology has had a particularly dramatic increase in importance in this period.

4. The influence of management writers

   Several American and U.K. studies and reports were produced during the 1980's which analyzed what made companies successful. These concluded that flexibility, customer orientation, a focus on quality and a strong sense of employee commitment to the organisation characterised these companies.

Overall these trends combined to create a shift away from traditional industrial relations based personnel management towards new techniques which became labelled as human resource management. A comparison of the two approaches is shown below:

Personnel/IR	HRM
Advisory and administrative	Strategic
Personnel activity in the organisation is marginalised and not seen as central to the corporate plan	HR activity in the organisation is fundamentally linked to the corporate plan
Few personnel directors on the Board	An HR director is essential on the Board
Personnel as a mediating role between management and the workforce	HRM as a central management role
Personnel as a specialist activity	HRM as a generalist activity
Emphasis on written rules and procedures	Flexibility more important than systems
Collective rewards and benefits	Individual rewards and benefits
Tightly defined jobs	Loosely defined jobs
Conflict built into the system by collective bargaining and negotiation	Conflict minimised through consultation and participation
A command and control management hierarchy	A team-based management system

Many of the HRM techniques are associated with successful Japanese and American companies and their systems of management.

To summarise, therefore, it is difficult to produce one general interpretation of what HRM means today. For each organisation the techniques and methods used will differ. In reality organisations can rarely be labelled as using either pure personnel/IR or HRM techniques a mixture of both of them is much more usual.

1.3 Human resource management roles and policies

As indicated in the previous section it is difficult to generalise about the roles and activities associated with HRM. Each organisation will differ in the number and range of activities performed, and in the balance it desires between general management and specialist HRM control. One early definition of personnel management makes the inter-relationship between line and specialist roles clear:

Personnel is a responsibility of all those who manage people, as well as being a description of the work of those who are employed as specialists. It is that part of management concerned with people at work and their relationship within the enterprise.

(IPM 1963)

Traditionally, many larger organisations had a strong central HRM department which was responsible for formulating policy and contained individuals with specialist expertise. This central HRM department provided advice and guidance and ensured standardisation of behaviour between the line managers. Line managers were responsible for the day-to-day handling of employees within a framework of rules and procedures. This pattern led to the creation of large, central HRM departments supporting a network of colleagues in the field. HRM activity was advisory and bureaucratic involving much record keeping and form filling.

The economic pressures of the 1980's and '90's as shown in the previous section, progressively altered this pattern of activity in many organisations. More of the operational HRM activities have been "returned to the line" to allow managers more individual control over staffing and productivity. Line managers are no longer constrained by systems and procedures and can operate more flexibly. They are, however, also more accountable for success or failure as there is often only a small central control function to support them.

Various commentators have argued that HRM jobs have also changed to reflect these trends. There are fewer administrative jobs in HRM, but more top-level strategic jobs, and an increased role for HRM consultants both from within and outside the organisation.

Activity

From the list of HRM activities below, indicate which you feel would be performed by a line manager, which would be performed by an HRM director, and which would be performed by a consultant?

☐ operator training

☐ formulating a human resource management plan

☐ psychometric assessment

☐ selecting a clerical worker

☐ conducting a disciplinary interview

You may have had some difficulty in deciding between the 3 alternatives in this activity. Often the degree to which the activity is shared by all managers or devolved to a specialist consultant or HRM director is a matter of organisational choice. Broadly, operator training and clerical selection would normally be seen as a line activity, psychometric assessment as a consultant activity, and formulating human resource management plans as a director's activity. The disciplinary interview could be conducted by any one of them depending on company policy.

In general the day-to-day management activities will be performed by line managers, with activities requiring specialist knowledge and expertise conducted by consultants. HRM directors formulate the overall HR strategy and ensure that HR policies are created to implement it.

Human resource management policies provide guidelines on what should be done within the organisation, and define rules of behaviour. Policies are therefore, very important in establishing the ground rules on how members of the organisation conduct themselves. Policies also help ensure consistency and fairness of treatment for all. They form a framework within which all members of the organisation operate.

Policies can be formulated for many areas but most organisations will have a general HRM policy stating the attitude of the organisation to the people it employs.

This will normally include ideas about fairness or equality of treatment, statements on the quality of working life, and on working conditions and security of labour. Following on from these general principles more detailed policies on specific areas may be constructed covering selection, promotion, training, health and safety, terms and conditions of employment and employee relations areas.

Examples of extracts from HRM policy statements are:

❒ All vacancies will be advertised within the organisation as well as externally.

❒ The organisation will only negotiate with recognised trade unions.

❒ Every employee has the right to equality of opportunity in selection for employment.

❒ The company intends to achieve the highest possible standards of health and safety in the workplace.

Policies will then be translated into practice by devising procedures to implement them. An example is shown below of the disciplinary procedure (small firms) produced by ACAS (Advisory, Conciliation and Arbitration Service):

Disciplinary procedure

(1) *Purpose and scope*

The Company's aim is to encourage improvement in individual conduct. This procedure sets out the action which will be taken when disciplinary rules are breached.

(2) *Principles*

a) The procedure is designed to establish the facts quickly and to deal consistently with disciplinary issues. No disciplinary action will be taken until the matter has been fully investigated.

b) At every stage employees will have the opportunity to state their case and be represented, if they wish, at the hearings by a shop steward if appropriate, or by a fellow employee.

c) An employee has the right to appeal against any disciplinary penalty.

(3) *The Procedure*

Stage 1 – Oral warning

If conduct or performance is unsatisfactory, the employee will be given a formal ORAL WARNING, which will be recorded. The warning will be disregarded after ...... months satisfactory service.

Stage 2 – Written warning

If the offence is serious, if there is no improvement in standards, or if a further offence occurs, a WRITTEN WARNING will be given which will include the reason for the warning and a note that, if there is no improvement after ...... months, a final written warning will be given.

Stage 3 – Final written warning

If conduct or performance is still unsatisfactory, A FINAL WRITTEN WARNING will be given making it clear that any recurrence of the offence or other serious misconduct within a period of ...... months will result in dismissal.

Stage 4 – Dismissal

If there is no satisfactory improvement or if further serious misconduct occurs, the employee will be DISMISSED.

Gross misconduct

If, after investigation, it is confirmed that an employee has committed an offence of the following nature (the list is not exhaustive), the normal consequence will be dismissal:

> theft, damage to company property, fraud, incapacity for work due to being under the influence of alcohol or illegal drugs, physical assault and gross insubordination.

While the alleged gross misconduct is being investigated the employee may be suspended, during which time he or she will be paid the normal hourly rate. Any decision to dismiss will be taken by the employer only.

(4) *Appeals*

An employee who wishes to appeal against any disciplinary decision must do so to the employer within two working days. The employer will hear the appeal and decide the case as impartially as possible.

Policies and procedures will not be effective unless they are communicated to others. The policy needs to be publicised and suitable training and support given in how it is to be implemented. The success of the policy should be monitored and modifications made if necessary.

Activity

Devise a policy statement about an employee's right to confidentiality when providing personal details to be held on computer file. Having devised the policy then write out the accompanying procedures to implement it.

Although the wording may vary your policy statement would be something like:

☐ All information provided by an employee will be treated as confidential. This means that it will be used only for the purpose indicated, and no unauthorised individual will be allowed access at any time. Disclosure of confidential information is a disciplinary offence.

Procedures to implement this policy would need to ensure the accurate input of data, the use of a security clearance system to allow data to be extracted, and the right of the individual under the Data Protection Act to examine his/her own computerised records.

1.4 Human resource management and the external environment

Just as HRM must be in tune with other organisational systems, so it must be aware of the constraints provided by the external environment. Employees are part of the wider social system and what happens at work will always be affected by what happens outside. At both local, national and international levels the impact of the following external factors on HRM will need to be analyzed:

❏ the social environment – including demographic trends of birth/death rates, mobility patterns, male/female activity rates, education patterns, skills profiles and trade union membership;

❏ the political environment – including the effects of local, national and international political policies and philosophies in general, and the operation of the public sector in particular (ie privatisation v state ownership etc);

❏ the legal environment – including the degree to which employment issues are regulated by law, and the potential conflicts in the U.K. between national and E.U. legal traditions;

❏ the economic environment – arguably the most important, in terms of growth/recession, the structure of the economy between primary/manufacturing/service sectors, levels of employment/unemployment etc;

❏ the technological environment – the sophistication of the technology in use and its consequences for employment patterns, together with the training, skills and expertise required for its effective utilisation.

Internationally, the U.K. system is increasingly seen as fundamentally linked with that of our European neighbours, particularly through membership of the European Union (E.U.) The Single European Act ensured that from the 1st January 1993 restrictions on the free passage of finance and labour throughout the member states would be reduced. This obviously affects labour supply and creates new opportunities and threats. European legislation is also affecting U.K. policy, and closer economic links encourage companies to expand across national boundaries. Other trading blocs, such as the U.S.A. and the Pacific rim countries continue to provide powerful challenges to the U.K. economy, and the break-up of the former Soviet Union provides another significant feature of the international economy. All these influences will affect domestic HRM strategies. HRM specialists cannot afford to be insular and inward-looking if they hope to compete in the international economy.

At the national level, the HRM specialist would have to be aware of the labour market for professional and senior management staff. Re-location issues and disparities between regions will affect mobility and salary levels. Government subsidies for particular areas could also influence decisions on plant location.

At the local level, any factor affecting the supply of labour would be important. The local unemployment rate, skills available and presence of competitors will all be affected by the local market rates. Travel patterns and road and rail networks will also help determine local labour supply.

You are the HR manager for Yelcom a medium sized electronics company based in West Germany. The company employs a full range of managerial, skilled and unskilled staff. Yelcom are considering opening a new plant in the U.K. in Swindon, and you have been asked to carry out an analysis to establish what the major factors affecting HRM in this area would be. List the issues that you would need to investigate.

You should not have had too much difficulty with this activity if you used the checklist provided as your model. When analyzing the social environment you would need to investigate the local labour force in terms of the skills available, educational output, unemployment rates, availability of transport, housing provision, and male/female activity rates. Nationally, the labour force for professional and managerial staff would need to be established together with the market rates for wages/salaries in the area. Politically, the availability of grants and local authority support for new business would be relevant, together with the political reaction to inward investment in the country. Legally, the U.K. employment law requirements would need to be fully understood, and locally any constraints on the development of the site would need to be investigated. Economically, the presence of other competitors in the region, business start-ups/closures, the availability of finance, transport and distribution networks would all be important factors. Technologically, the availability of skilled staff to work with Yelcom's technology, and the organisational requirements to maximise business efficiency would need to be assessed.

1.5 Human resource management as a profession

An important debate relating to human resource management is the degree to which specialists in this field can be said to form a profession in common with other functional areas such as law or finance. The definition of a professional is not a straightforward one. Some commentators use it to denote an efficient worker who uses expertise, whereas others use it in a far more restricted sense to denote those who belong to an association which regulates entry and gives exclusive rights to practice. Law and medicine come into this latter category but HRM does not even though there is a recognised professional association the Institute of Personnel and Development (I.P.D.)

In effect the debate is fairly academic, but HRM does suffer a lack of credibility in some quarters because the standards of professional practice are less distinct that those of medicine, law or accountancy.

Consider the duties and responsibilities of a chartered accountant in an organisation and those of the human resource manager. What do you believe are the characteristics each must possess to be considered professional?

For the chartered accountant your reply probably included the idea that to be professional the calculations and financial information provided should be accurate and in accordance with recognised standards. The accountant's role is to ensure good accounting systems, providing suitable controls, are in place. Probably, you also included membership of a professional accounting body in your definition. For the human resource manager, to be professional means that the manager is competent and expert at his/her role and contributes positively to the organisation in establishing effective people management systems. It is unlikely that membership of the I.P.D. would be seen as an absolute requirement to practise as a human resource manager.

1.6 Summary

In this chapter the essential elements required to understand the role human resource management plays in an organisation have been outlined. Human resource managers need to be focused both internally to ensure people management systems complement other organisational systems, and externally to make sure HRM techniques match the requirements of the business environment.

Further reading

Armstrong M. *A Handbook of Personnel Management Practice*, Kogan Page Ltd, 1984, Part 1.

Cole G.A. *Personnel Management* (3rd edition), DP Publications 1993, Chapters 1-3.

Farnham D, *Personnel in Context* (3rd edition), IPM Publications 1990

Storey J (ed) *New Perspectives on Human Resource Management*, Routledge 1989, Chapters 1-5.

Sisson K, *Personnel Management in Britain*, Blackwells 1989, Chapters 1-2.

Torrington D and Hall L, *Personnel Management: a new approach*, Prentice Hall International (UK) Ltd 1987, Chapters 1-3.

Exercises

Progress questions

These questions have been designed to help you remember the key points in this chapter. The answers to the questions are on p124

Complete the following sentences:

1. The welfare tradition is based on the belief that...

2. Scientific management was the term used to describe...

3. Industrial relations is primarily concerned with ....

4. Characterisitcs of the personnel management approach include..

5. Characteristics of HRM include...

Select the correct response to the following statements:

6. HRM is a specialist activity.

True ☐ False ☐

7. HRM is an integral part of the corporate plan of the organisation.

True ☐ False ☐

8. HRM is fundamentally affected by the external environment.

True ☐ False ☐

9. All HRM specialists must be member of the professional institute (IPD).

True ☐ False ☐

10. HRM is most effective if controlled centrally by the organisation.

True ☐ False ☐

Review questions

These questions have been designed to help you check your comprehension of the key points in this chapter. You may wish to look further than the text in this chapter in order to answer them fully. You will find your library useful as a source of wider reading. You can check the essential elements of your answers by referring to the appropriate section.

11. How would you describe the traditions and techniques that make up HRM today? (Section 1.2)

12. What were the main factors in the 1980's that led to a move away from traditional industrial relations led personnel management? (Section 1.2)

13. What are the main external factors that impact upon the HRM function? (Section 1.4)

14. Discuss the extent to which HRM is a specialist or generalist activity (Section 1.3 and 1.5)

Multiple choice questions

The answers to these questions are given in the Lecturer's Supplement.

15. The main professional institute for human resource management is:
    a) the I.C.S.A
    b) the I.P.M.
    c) the I.T.D.
    d) the I.P.D

16. A study of demographic trends would be part of the analysis of the:
    a) economic environment
    b) social environment
    c) political environment
    d) legal environment

17. Which of the following is not normally associated with an HRM approach:
    a) individualised reward systems
    b) team working
    c) collective bargaining
    d) job flexibility

Practice questions

A marking guide to these questions is given in the Lecturer's Supplement.

18. Describe some of the international influences on HRM.

19. How can changes in the social environment of the country affect HRM?

20. Outline the main differences between a personnel/IR approach and an HRM approach.

21. What is the function of personnel policies and procedures, and what areas do they normally cover?

22. How has the role of the HR function changed over time?

Questions for advanced students

A marking guide to these questions is given in the Lecturer's Supplement.

23. Consider an organisation where you have had work experience or any other with which you are familiar. What personnel policies and procedures were there in operation and how effectively were they monitored?

24. What areas would an audit of the HR function need to cover to establish its effectiveness?

Assignment: Making Headway

A marking guide to this assignment is given in the Lecturer's Supplement.

Headway Estate Agents are a regional chain of 20 outlets based in the south-west of England. During the housing boom of the 1970's and early 1980's they expanded rapidly from the original two offices in Exeter, to 35 branches in the south-west by 1985. The recession and decline in the housing market in the late 1980's and early 1990's affected Headway badly, in common with much of the housing industry, and 15 offices were subsequently closed.

Traditionally, Headway has been a family-run, rather paternalistic business, with great loyalty from the staff and low turnover. The branch closures caused a shock throughout the organisation and the realisation that more efficient working practices were needed in the future. The managing director has now decided to appoint a specialist human resource manager for the first time, with responsibility for co-ordinating and developing HR policy.

Required

As advisor to the managing director, discuss:

i) the content of the new HR manager's job;

ii) what environmental factors need to be assessed in order to establish their effects on HRM in the future.

2 The organisational context

2.1 Introduction

This chapter looks at the various ways organisations operate and the way this influences HRM. The chapter starts by looking at organisational design and structure and explores the idea of "the flexible firm". It then moves on to look at managerial systems and how these contribute to organisational culture. The chapter ends with a broad consideration of the link between motivation, job satisfaction, and work productivity.

This chapter covers some of the elements in the "create, maintain and enhance effective working relationships" unit of the MCI management standards.

On completing this chapter you should be able to:

❐ understand how organisational structure affects management systems and work design

❐ explain how to build flexibility into work systems

❐ understand how management systems and style help determine organisational culture

❐ analyse the link between motivation, job satisfaction and work efficiency.

2.2 Organisational design and structure

We saw in the previous chapter that human resource management is just one part of the whole organisation's management systems and that the HRM role is affected by the overall design and structure of the organisation. Organisational structures rarely start from scratch, usually they evolve and change over time to respond to the needs of the external environment and create new opportunities within the organisation. One of the key challenges for an organisation is to ensure that the structure of the organisation meets its current and future purpose and strategic needs.

One of the crucial elements of this process is the balance that must be maintained between the need to divide up work into manageable tasks which can be allocated to particular work groups and the need to retain a common sense of purpose and ensure those de-centralised tasks can be integrated again effectively. The larger the organisation the greater the complexity of both dividing and integrating work.

In the human resource management area the same issues of de-centralising or centralising operations occur.

Activity

Consider a national supermarket chain such as Tesco, Sainsburys, Asda or Waitrose. What aspects of HRM work do you believe are best organised centrally and which might be better if de-centralised? Give your reasons.

Although this is ultimately a matter of organisational choice, generally areas such as pay, promotion and the upholding of employment law would be managed centrally, with recruitment and selection, training and distribution of personnel handled regionally or locally. The advantage of centralised control is consistency and fairness of treatment together with the ability to develop specialist expertise, the advantage of decentralised systems are the greater local knowledge and responses of the managers. Ideally, systems that combine the best of both can be put in place.

One way in which an organisation can attempt to create a sense of common purpose and ensure that HRM and other functional plans integrate with corporate strategy is by communicating a "vision" of the future direction of the organisation. This vision is then translated into "mission statements" which set out the key tasks for the organisation which can be sub-divided into the mission of each department or function.

Organisational structures and work teams can be built around a variety of groupings including:

❒ functions

❒ geographical areas

❒ products

❒ time periods (shifts)

❒ customer bases (retail/wholesale)

❒ technology (mass-production/small batch etc)

Activity

Try to identify one example of the use of each of the above structural groupings.

Functional groupings are normally used for specialist activities, so the grouping relates to particular work skills or knowledge. Examples include accounting, marketing, and the HRM function itself. Geographical groupings are common in retail chains where a number of outlets are combined in regional areas. Product differentiation is more common in manufacturing areas or in financial services where departments are created around a particular brand or type of account. Time period or shift differentiation, occurs in organisations which operate over extended hours or even 24 hour time periods such as manufacturing or public services such as hospitals, police forces or fire services etc Employees may be grouped into shift teams. Divisions based on customer type occur in many supplier industries particularly in food, clothing and electrical goods.

Finally, technology grouped structures may occur in manufacturing or chemical processing organisations.

Other factors which determine organisational structure include the number of levels in the management hierarchy and the span of control of each manager. These issues are explored further in section 3.4.

One of the most important current issues for many organisations is designing flexibility into the structure of the organisation. There are two main ways this can be done:

❒ task flexibility

❒ time flexibility

Task flexibility involves organising work into multi-tasked jobs rather than rigidly defined jobs. The emphasis is more on work teams where the individuals are interchangeable rather than the more traditional hierarchical supervision structures. Individuals in the work team do what is needed to achieve the work objectives, they have more freedom to organise individually how this is done. The responsibility for performing is focused less on the team leader and more on the whole team's efforts. The implications of this for job analysis are explored in section 3.4 and the process of setting team objectives is covered in section 7.2.

Time flexibility is based on the idea of matching working hours more closely to the demands of the job, rather than paying individuals simply to be at the workplace. This can be achieved by using a wider variety of work contracts, or by re-organising the way the employee's hours are worked.

Flexibility can be built into employment contracts by:

1. using fixed-term contracts rather than permanent contracts;

2. using part-time variable contracts rather than full-time fixed hours contracts;

3. using contract or agency staff rather than employing individuals directly.

Flexibility can be built into the way hours are organised by:

1. flexi-time (having variable start and finish times);

2. annual hours (measuring hours worked over a whole year rather than by the week);

3. shift patterns;

4. compressed working week (working longer hours per day but fewer days per week or fortnight).

Activity

Seasonal products such as ice-cream or Easter eggs require a highly flexible labour force that can be employed swiftly when demand is high and then removed once demand falls. How can an organisation structure its staff to accommodate this?

Suggestions include:

1. if there are other product lines as well, staff could be moved around the organisation to fill whatever need was the most urgent;

2. part-time staff could be employed for a few hours per week all year on the understanding that considerable additional hours will be worked in periods of peak demand;

3. staff could be employed on annual hours contracts and the hours allocated to the peak demand period, but paid monthly;

4. temporary staff could be recruited on fixed term contracts to cover the peak demand period.

The strategy adopted would depend to a large extent on the skills required in the job, and the availability of suitable labour. Human resource planning for these situations is the subject of the next chapter.

2.3 Managerial systems and organisational culture

As we have already seen the structure of the organisation will partly determine what managers are expected to do, and the way work and teams are organised. As well as the structure, however, other managerial systems will also affect how the organisation operates.

Management systems can be subdivided into:

❑ control systems

❑ information systems

❑ people systems

Control systems are concerned with collecting data, comparing it with standards or targets and undertaking corrective action if necessary. The way controls are imposed tells you a lot about the organisation. Some have very rigid and complex monitoring systems and procedures, these may not necessarily be the most effective, however. Feedback needs to be immediate, non-judgemental and acted upon quickly to ensure a deviation is corrected before a problem becomes significant.

Information systems are essential for a healthy organisation. Communication systems should ensure the right information is available to individuals to allow them to be able to achieve their objectives. Increased use of technology has dramatically changed the way information is transmitted, and the speed at which it is available. Employees no longer need to be within close proximity to each other to communicate, the telephone, fax and e-mail have speeded up long distance communication considerably. Managers are able, with the help of computers, to process more data and monitor more individual's work performance than ever before.

People systems are the main focus of this text, and cover a wide variety of ways of controlling behaviour in the organisation. Selection, training, promotion, reward, discipline, planning, negotiation and many other processes all regulate the people in the organisation.

To be effective studies have indicated that managers need to have a combination of 3 skill sets:

❑ human, the interpersonal skills;

❑ technical, the decision/knowledge skills;

❑ conceptual, the planning, visionary skills.

The MCI personal competence model shown in section 6.3 identifies these factors in greater detail.

Many managers have a preference for one of these areas more than the others, this is sometimes referred to as their management style. People-centred managers excel in the inter-personal skills area, others are more technical and task focused, others more conceptual. Organisations may actively promote one of these areas more than the others, and evolve a "culture" which has a preference for a particular style.

Culture has been described as "the way we do things around here" and is a complex mix of organisational and inter-personal factors. Historical traditions and influential founders/senior managers can set the tone of the organisation, and the

HRM function can be seen as highly important in maintaining or developing the culture of the organisation. Through recruitment and selection, reward management systems and appraisal the desired behaviour can be re-inforced.

Characteristics of the McDonald's corporation include common colours, logo's and restaurant layouts worldwide, fast service, uniformed employees and a standardised range of products. The customer care style reflected in staff behaviour and attitude is also standardised throughout the outlets.

Management systems of planning, decision-making, and communicating will underpin the culture. Where consultation is invited, work methods are flexible and the management style is "people centred" a more open culture is likely to exist. Where management control is more authoritarian, work methods more constrained and management style "task centred" a more closed culture will pervade.

2.4 *Motivation, job satisfaction and work productivity*

As shown by the previous sections motivation and job satisfaction at work are a complex mix of the following factors:

❑ the organisational structure and context;

❑ the work team and management relationships;

❑ the job itself.

Motivation results from the relationships and rewards provided by being in the working environment and the content of the job itself.

Theories of motivation suggest that individuals who have a clear sense of their own contribution to the organisation and who receive effective feedback from their managers and peers are more likely to experience job satisfaction than those who do not. Achieving goals and being recognised for doing so is intrinsically motivating.

Money or financial rewards are one method used to motivate staff, but financial rewards alone are rarely sufficient to provide job satisfaction. These issues will be explored in more depth in chapter 7.

The content of the job is also important. Effective work design can enhance motivation and lead to greater job satisfaction.

In the early part of the 20th century ideas derived from the scientific management tradition proposed that work should be divided into small, specialist tasks that could be repeated rapidly and which required minimal training or individual input. These ideas were made reality in the mass production assembly lines of many manufacturing organisations of the time. Clerical and office work could also be considered as another assembly line with staff performing just one element of a complex task.

Activity

What might be the likely consequences of requiring employees to perform simple, repetitive tasks all day and every day?

Employees become bored and alienated from the work they are doing, this can cause aggression and has resulted in deliberate vandalism of machinery. Stress caused by boredom can also lead to illness and absenteeism.

Activity

How could these de-motivating effects be modified?

Various techniques have been proposed to reduce alienation including job-rotation where a variety of tasks are performed rather than just one. Frequent rest breaks may ease the monotony, as could the provision of music or radio broadcasts whilst you work. Higher pay rates or bonuses have also been used to encourage workers to stick with the tasks.

The link between job satisfaction and work performance is complex. A key question is "is productivity directly related to being happy at work?" Some commentators suggest that employees may be happy if they have un-stressed, varied jobs with lots of opportunity for inter-personal contact, but the organisation may suffer from a lack of business efficiency as a result. The challenge today is to combine both efficiency and job satisfaction.

2.5 Summary

In this chapter the essential elements needed to understand how organisations affect individuals at work have been covered. The chapter began by looking at how organisational structure and design affects the people working within it, and covered some of the ways organisations have attempted to become more flexible in their HR systems. The use of various management systems of control and communications was covered and the idea of management style was introduced. Finally, corporate culture was discussed and the link between job productivity and motivation debated.

Further reading

Drucker P, *The Practice of Management*, Heinemann, London 1954

Handy C, *Understanding Organisations*, Penguin 1993

Hunt J, *Managing People at Work* (3rd edition) McGraw Hill, 1992

Huczynski A & Buchanan D, *Organisational Behaviour* (2nd edition), Prentice Hall 1991

Mintzberg H, *The Nature of Managerial Work*, Harper and Row, New York 1973

Quinn R E et al, *Becoming a Master Manager*, John Wiley and Sons, New York 1990

Schein E, *Organisational Culture and Leadership*, Jossey-Bass, San Francisco, 1985

Exercises

Progress questions

These questions have been designed to help you remember the key points in this chapter. The answers to the questions are on p124

Complete the following sentences:

1. The mission statements of the organisation are ....

2. Work teams can be created around a variety of grouping including ....

3. Task flexibility is..

4. The management control systems of an organisation aim to...

5. The 3 skill sets needed by a manager are...

Select the correct responses to the following statements:

6. The advantage of centralised control is consistency and fairness of treatment and the ability to develop specialist expertise.

    True ☐ False ☐

7. Using fixed-term contracts is a form of task flexibility.

    True ☐ False ☐

8. Scientific management was a way of increasing labour productivity.

    True ☐ False ☐

9. Functional groupings are based on the products of the organisation.

    True ☐ False ☐

10. Task flexibility is the same as job rotation.

    True ☐ False ☐

Review questions

These questions have been designed to help you check your comprehension of the key points in this chapter. You may wish to look further than the text in this chapter in order to answer them fully. You will find your library useful as a source of wider reading. You can check the essential elements of your answers by referring to the appropriate section.

11. What are the main factors affecting organisational design? (Section 2.2)

12. Describe the main characteristics of task and time flexibility. (Section 2.2)

13. What are the main management systems and how do they relate to the overall organisational culture? (Section 2.3)

14. What did the scientific management theorists discover about the links between work productivity and job satisfaction? (Section 2.4)

Multiple choice questions

The answers to these questions are given in the Lecturer's Supplement.

15. An annual hours contract is:
    a) a fixed term contract of 1 year
    b) a way of measuring hours worked over a year rather than by the week
    c) a system where more hours are worked each day in order for fewer days to be worked per week/fortnight
    d) a system of variable start and finish times each day

16. Which of the following ideas are associated with scientific management?
    a) multi-task, flexible working
    b) autonomous group working
    c) task specialisation and work measurement

17. Which of the following is a characteristic of a traditional work contract?:
    a) variable hours
    b) fixed term
    c) fixed hours

18. Which of the following is a disadvantage of de-centralisation?:
    a) greater local knowledge
    b) contribution of line managers
    c) immediate reaction to events
    d) specialist advice

Practice questions

A marking guide to these questions is given in the Lecturer's Supplement.

19. What are the vision and mission statements of an organisation and what do they hope to achieve?

20. Around what methods of grouping employees can organisational structures be based?

21. What are the main methods of time flexibility, and how can they be used in an organisation?

22. What factors motivate employees at work and create job satisfaction?

Questions for advanced students

A marking guide to these questions is given in the Lecturer's Supplement.

23. How can you evaluate an organisation's current culture and how can the culture of an organisation be changed over time?

24. To what extent have changes in information technology affected the way organisations are structured?

Assignment: Work design difficulties at Compu-serve data processing bureau.

A marking guide to this assignment is given in the Lecturer's Supplement.

Compu-serve data processing bureau provides a mail order service for many organisations who wish to distribute circulars throughout the U.K. After each dispatch a proportion of the circulars are returned "not known at this address" and the details have to be checked against computer records and amended or deleted accordingly. Returns are batched in 100's and 8 data-processing operators amend the records for 7 hours each day.

Turnover and absenteeism is extremely high in this work group, and the supervisor finds it very hard to ensure that the daily work targets are met.

Required

As the HR manager:

1. give the supervisor advice on why you believe the data-processing operators are reacting in this way;

2. make recommendations on how this situation can be improved.

3 Human resource planning and administration

3.1 Introduction

This chapter looks at the human resource planning process and describes how it attempts to ensure the effective utilisation of staff by making sure the right number of people with the right skills are available to the organisation at all times. HR planning involves constructing short, medium and long term plans and ensuring the necessary analysis is undertaken and records kept to provide data for these plans. This chapter covers the "future personnel requirements" element of the Management NVQ's.

On completing this chapter you should be able to:

❑ understand the basis on which human resource plans are constructed and be able to interpret them;

❑ describe how to analyze the external labour market and be aware of sources of statistical data;

❑ construct a job description and carry out a job analysis;

❑ interpret data on a human resource management record system, and be aware of the requirements of the Data Protection Act (1984).

3.2 Human resource planning

The concept of planning for the present and future needs of the organisation is fundamental to the effective use of employees, yet many organisations find this a difficult process in reality. The requirements of today and the need to handle current crises, often distract general managers and human resource managers from standing back and taking a longer term view. Consequently, management is often criticised for "fire-fighting" and merely reacting to change, rather than anticipating it. The consequences of ineffective planning could be absorbed in the more buoyant economic conditions of the 1970's and early 1980's, but with recession and the severe economic difficulties of the late 1980's and 1990's many organisations have suffered badly from this failure to plan ahead.

Today the business environment continues to change rapidly, and the most successful organisations are those that can adapt quickly and react flexibly to the conditions of the 1990's and beyond.

The challenge for the HRM specialist is to help the organisation develop this flexibility through adequate HR planning. The time period over which the plan is formulated is the first key decision. Organisations differ in terms of the rapidity of change they experience, so in some cases planning is easily possible over a 2-3 year period, for others even 6 month's ahead is confused and uncertain. If a plan is to have any real value, however, it needs to consider not only the immediate short-term but also the medium term. For skills development a training period will obviously need to be built in to the plans, and this could be anything from a few months to several years. Most organisations try to produce a detailed 6 month to 1 year short term plan, set within a more general 2-5 year medium-term plan.

Human resource plans must be linked with the corporate plan of the organisation to be effective. The future needs of the organisation must be assessed in terms of both numbers of employees and their skills. Current levels of employment within the organisation must be monitored, and promotion and succession plans developed. Employees must also be trained and developed to ensure a constant supply of skills. Finally, labour efficiency and productivity data must be recorded to ensure efficient utilisation of staff.

Forecasting future demand for labour can be assisted by both qualitative and quantitative methods. In qualitative terms many organisations use the experience and judgement of their line mangers as the basis for forecasting labour demands. Managers submit the numbers and skill requirements for their departments for the next period (6 months/1 year), and these are then combined to form the organisation's short-term plan. This approach is sometimes referred to as the "bottom-up" method. Other organisations, perhaps more pressurised by financial constraints, plan for labour by deciding the overall budget and then allocating it downwards department by department (the "top-down" approach). In reality a combination of both methods may be the best compromise. Plans will be more effective when the information given in the corporate plan is detailed and managers are kept informed of future changes.

Demand forecasting can also be assisted by more quantitative methods. The main systems either use statistical trend/ratio analyses or other work study methods. Ratio/trend analysis involves looking at past performance records in order to predict future requirements. The following activity will illustrate this:

Activity

Busy burger bar has 25 outlets of almost identical size and structure in the south-west of England. Analysis suggests that a ratio of 1 waiter/waitress is needed for every 20 customers. How many staff are needed at the Taunton branch during the lunchtime period, if an average of 100 customers are served each day?

This is a very straightforward calculation which produces the requirement for 5 staff for this period, (100 customers ÷ 20 ratio)

In reality estimates are normally based on a complex set of inter-relationships and sophisticated computer models have been used by larger organisations to help with these calculations. General trends/ratios are often less helpful than those for specific groups of employees.

Other work study techniques involve timing particular operations then building back these results into estimates of the numbers of operators needed and their skills levels.

In the medium-term plan the detailed budget requirements of the short-term are developed into a more general picture of how the organisation wishes to develop in the future. Job and department re-organisations, mergers or sell-offs would all need longer-term planning. Promotion patterns and future skills requirements must also be assessed in the longer term. The details may be less precise, but the overall needs will be included. Also important is the continual review of actual requirements against projections. Any significant problem in forecasting needs to be analyzed to try to ensure it doesn't happen again.

When analyzing the current labour force the strategy the organisation uses to staff its jobs will be important. Some organisations regularly bring in new staff at all levels of the organisation, others prefer to appoint new staff at junior levels only and then train and develop them internally. Others use a mixture of the two approaches.

When analyzing internal labour supply for the HR plan it is essential firstly that adequate records are held (see section 3.5). The numbers and type of leavers and joiners, promotion patterns and job changes all need to be recorded. Leaving patterns are normally analyzed both statistically and individually to determine what is going on. One basic statistical measure is the annual labour turnover index.

This is calculated in the following way:

$$\frac{\text{Number of leavers in the year}}{\text{Average number of staff employed in the year}} \times 100$$

The annual labour turnover index is a relatively crude measure because it doesn't discount the staff who join and leave the company within the year. Turnover is more significant for key staff or those who have been with the organisation for longer periods. Therefore, annual labour turnover calculations are more informative if applied to particular categories of staff, or staff of different ages. The calculations can also be useful to help the organisation make comparisons between one year and another, or between one work group and another.

Activity

Based on the statistics for employees at the Speedy Save discount warehouses shown below, calculate the annual labour turnover index:

1. for the organisation as whole;

2. for the senior managers/directors.

	Total number employed	Number of leavers
Senior managers/directors	4	3
Managers	15	1
Supervisors	20	2
Clerical staff	150	16
Semi-skilled staff	110	6
Manual staff	70	5
Total	369	33

Annual labour turnover index for the whole staff is 8.94% (33 ÷ 369 × 100)

Turnover of senior managers is 75% (3 ÷ 4 × 100), a much more worrying feature of employment.

A separate measure, the stability index, discounts staff with less than 1 year's service. The stability index is calculated as follows:

$$\frac{\text{Number of staff with 1 year's service or more}}{\text{Number of staff employed 1 year ago}} \times 100$$

Other analysis techniques involve conducting individual exit interviews to explore the reasons why staff are leaving. Cohort analysis may be used to track the progress through the organisation of a group who joined at the same time. Possible groups include management trainees, sales staff etc As these studies may cover many years, sometimes a "half-life" analysis is used where the group is studied up to the point where half of them have left. Retention profiles may also be plotted to show how many people remain with the organisation by age group or occupation.

The extent of the analyses made depends partly on the degree to which the organisation invests in and develops its internal labour force. There may not be a particular problem in having high labour turnover providing the staff are easily available and require little training. High levels of turnover for key staff is obviously more worrying, as is a sudden leap in turnover rates.

Analyzing the supply of labour from the external market is the subject of the next section (3.3).

The final element of planning involves balancing demand and supply for labour if the current situation needs adjustment. This is where the flexibility requirement is important.

Activity

What could an organisation do if:

1. it finds it has too many workers in a particular area;
2. it finds it has too few workers in an area?

If the organisation has too many staff for current requirements, overtime will stop, staff may be "laid off" temporarily, no new staff would be recruited, and some individuals may be relocated to other sites/departments. Fixed term contracts may not be renewed, and staff could have their hours reduced if their contracts allowed. If the problem remains in the longer-term early retirements could be sought or voluntary redundancies. Ultimately, compulsory redundancies would be needed in severe cases.

Where staff are being actively sought in particular categories, the organisation could enhance salaries and benefits to attract applicants, and promote the vacancies more widely. Support methods such as creche facilities and term-time only contracts could be used to attract a wider range of applicants. Training programmes could be accelerated, or entry criteria lowered. Contract or agency staff could be used or ultimately the job could be re-designed or replaced by the use of other technologies.

Organisations where staff are trained in a range of skills allowing them to be moved around departments to meet demand is often the ultimate aim of the HR plan.

3.3 Labour market analysis

In the previous section we looked at the analysis of the internal labour market, in this section features of the external labour market will be explored.

As outlined in Chapter 1.4, the external environment and the external labour market can be analyzed at 3 levels, locally, nationally and internationally.

At the local level the available working population, its skills and education levels, unemployment figures and the presence of other competitors will all affect supply. Travel to work patterns and availability of housing will also affect the labour supply. Locally, there may be fairly significant geographical differences affecting the cost of living and availability of labour. London and the south east of England tend to have higher costs of living, a larger labour pool, some skills shortages and lower unemployment. Scotland, the north of England and Wales have experienced a more serious economic decline resulting in higher unemployment levels and lower wages. Regional variations may cause difficulties if relocation is desired, incentives may need to be paid, or regional allowances added to salaries.

Nationally, demographic changes and changes to the nature of the workforce are having significant effects. Demographically, the number of young people entering the workforce has dropped dramatically, in 1989 22% of the workforce were under 25, by 2000 this will be down to 17% Other age groups are expanding, the 35-54 age range in 1989 was approximately 41% of the workforce, by 2000 this is projected to rise to 47%.

Other features include greater numbers of women joining the workforce, and an increase in the number of part-time jobs.

The structure of the labour force is also changing with more people employed in the service sector, and less in the manufacturing and primary sectors.

Activity

The diagram below projects the general trends in employment since 1960 forward to the year 2000.

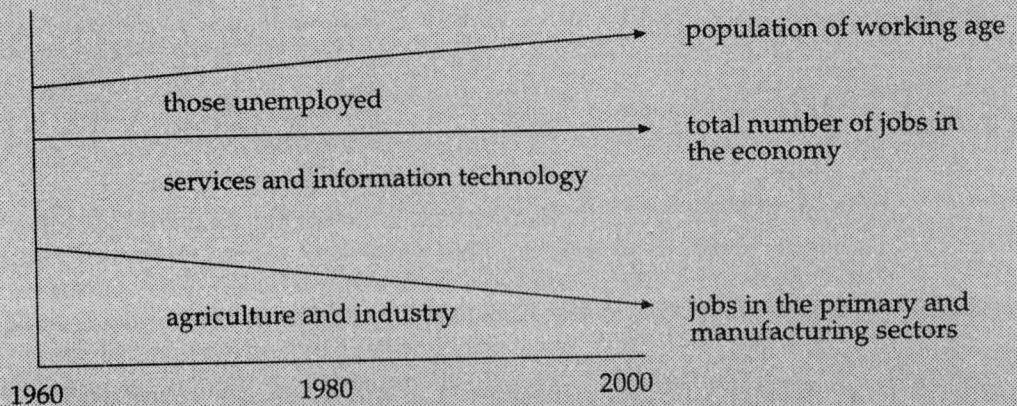

The population of working age has increased every year and is expected to continue to grow past the end of the century. The total number of jobs in the economy has remained relatively stable, although the numbers employed in the agriculture and industry sectors continues to decline and services and information increase.

What are the long term implications of these trends?

If the population of working age continues to increase but the total number of jobs in the economy doesn't, there will be more people wanting jobs than jobs available. The consequences could be ever higher unemployment. The economy needs to grow and expand every year in order to reduce this problem. Also, as total numbers of jobs in agriculture and industry decline, the service sector will have to continue to expand in order to even maintain current employment levels. If service sector growth levels off, the problems of employment could become worse.

Another feature affecting labour markets is the increased use of technology which allows more work to be done by the same number of employees. Computerisation and robotics have already transformed productivity rates in many areas and are partly responsible for reduced employment in agriculture and manufacturing.

Internationally, many of the same structural changes are affecting other European countries and the USA. Within the EC labour forces are more mobile allowing skilled and unskilled workers to be employed in other countries.

3.4 Job analysis and job design

Another important part of HR planning is organisational design and the design of individual jobs. Chapter 2.2 looked at the process of organisational design, so this section will look at job design and job analysis.

Job design involves 3 main stages:

1. establishing the relationships that should exist between the job holder and other members of the department or section;

2. deciding on the content of a job in terms of its duties and responsibilities;

3. determining the methods to be used in carrying out the job.

The first stage is to analyze what work needs to be done within the organisation in a particular department or section. For traditional organisations this usually involves setting up a hierarchy of jobs with specific job responsibilities attached to each, and clear responsibility differences between senior and junior posts. This was often represented in an organisation chart where the total workload was divided into sections and layers. An example of this structure is shown overleaf. It follows through one reporting line within the organisation:

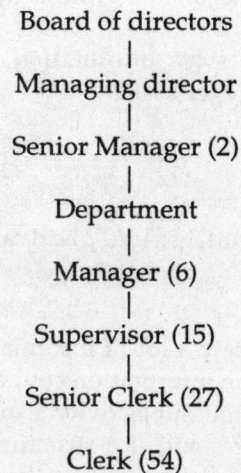

Board of directors
|
Managing director
|
Senior Manager (2)
|
Department
|
Manager (6)
|
Supervisor (15)
|
Senior Clerk (27)
|
Clerk (54)

Increasingly, this method of organising jobs has been criticised because it creates organisational rigidity and prevents flexibility. An alternative system uses generic jobs which contain a much wider range of tasks, and the levels within the organisation are reduced to produce a wider, flatter organisation chart.

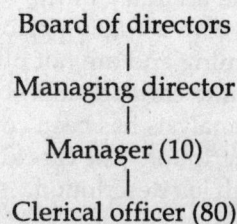

Board of directors
|
Managing director
|
Manager (10)
|
Clerical officer (80)

The structure of the organisation will affect the actual content of individual jobs. The process of collecting data about a job is normally referred to as job analysis.

If you had to analyze the duties and responsibilities of a supermarket produce manager's job at Sainsbury's, how might you collect the necessary information?

There are a range of methods that could be appropriate:

1. interview existing produce managers and ask them to tell you about their jobs;

2. interview the produce manager's boss and/or staff;

3. construct a questionnaire which could be filled in by produce managers at several stores;

4. ask selected produce managers to keep a work diary and record what they are doing over a period of weeks;

5. observe a produce manager at work;

6. actually do the job of a produce manager yourself;

7. refer to any store information or computer systems that told you about the produce manager's role.

What are the advantages and disadvantages of each method?

Interviews generate a lot of information and when based on a job holder the data is very relevant. The information could be biased, however, and not reflect all aspects of the job. Individual subjectivity can be modified by interviewing several different produce managers and if a structured interview plan is followed the data collected can be standardised. The picture the produce manager's boss has about the job should also be sought to confirm the basic details.

Questionnaires are useful if larger numbers of participants are needed, but the questions asked will need to be straightforward and unambiguous. A personal follow up with selected respondents can help validate the data.

Work diaries can be useful, but they rely upon the individual's willingness to fill them out, and the accuracy of the data is always difficult to assess. Observation and methods that involve actually performing the job tasks (participant observation), are very time consuming and are not often used in this type of analysis. Other sources of data can be useful to check details obtained by other methods.

Once the job analysis has been completed the information is often written up in the form of a job description. The checklist below should help you construct a well-organised and thorough job description.

1. Is the job description for an individual job, or is it part of a generic family of jobs? If individual, the job description will stand alone, if generic the job will form part of a ladder or family of job descriptions.

2. All job descriptions need an identification section which states the job title and reporting relationships. An effective way of communicating this is in an organisation chart which helps establish the relationships between this job and others.

3. The overall purpose of the job is normally stated in the form of a brief statement of why this job (or family of jobs) exists.

4. The principal accountabilities or key results areas of the job are then listed. Normally there will be between 4-10 broad job areas. For each key task further details about how the task is to be performed may be included, or for generic jobs the various skill levels may be defined.

5. A section outlining the nature and scope of the job may also be included to expand upon the details given in the first 4 sections. The object is to provide more background to the job requirements. This may be in a narrative format, or in further structured headings. The decision on the format depends partly on the nature of the job being analyzed, and partly on the style the organisation chooses to adopt.

    Possible areas to be covered by this section include:

    ❏ limits of authority

    ❏ resources available (ie plant, equipment and tools used)

    ❏ supervisory responsibilities

    ❏ contacts both within and outside the organisation

    ❏ financial statistics (ie costs, budgets, incomes, turnover etc)

    ❏ statistics on the number of customers, locations, production targets, sales etc

    ❏ physical working conditions

Activity

Write a job description that could be used for a family of jobs at different levels based on the work of a secretary.

A possible example of this type of generic job description is shown below:

JOB TITLE: Secretary

JOB LEVEL:

REPORTS TO:

SUPERVISES:

DATE:

. . . .

PURPOSE OF THE JOB

To provide an accurate and efficient secretarial service, meeting all deadlines and undertaking all administrative work as required.

KEY TASK AREAS

1.   Carry out typing and wordprocessing assignments quickly and accurately.

2.   Take shorthand dictation and transcribe accurately.

3.   Undertake audio-typing as required.

4.   Answer the telephone on behalf of the manager(s), and deal with personal callers.

5.   Make appointments, arrange meetings and manage the diary of the manager(s) concerned.

6.   Send FAX, Telex, E-mail or other messages as required.

7.   Maintain an accurate filing system.

LEVELS OF RESPONSIBILITY

Secretarial jobs are graded into three levels of responsibility according to the skills and experience required.

Level 1   The jobholder carries out routine secretarial duties under the close supervision of the manager or more senior secretarial staff. The individual is not expected to take the initiative or answer queries without consultation.

Level 2   The jobholder undertakes routine secretarial duties without supervision, but refers more complex items to a supervisor. Routine queries will be answered without reference to others, but more senior staff will be consulted on non-standard matters.

Level 3   The jobholder operates autonomously in most situations, substituting for the manager(s) concerned where necessary.

The final element of job design involves determining the methods by which the individual carries out his or her job. This involves deciding how much supervision is needed, and considering other elements associated with job enrichment. De-motivation occurs as a result of very rigid, mechanical work tasks. Job rotation may help increase worker satisfaction, or a greater emphasis on teamwork and interchanging roles. The newer, more generic, jobs can use more stimulating methods because of the greater flexibility in the content of the jobs.

3.5 Human resource management record systems

In order to plan effectively, the organisation must ensure it has detailed and up-to-date records on all employees. In the past these records were mostly kept in paper-based files, and extracting information was very time consuming. The introduction of computerised record systems and data bases has revolutionised the processing of information and provided much more effective methods of analysis.

Typical records on individual employees might include:

☐ personal details such as name, sex, date of birth, address, education, qualifications, previous experience, tax code, national insurance number, next of kin, disabilities etc;

☐ employment details such as the date employment began, the date the present job started, job title;

☐ details of terms and conditions of employment;

☐ absence details;

☐ details of any accidents;

☐ details of any disciplinary action taken;

☐ training records.

Personnel records may also provide collective information, for example:

☐ the numbers and occupations of employees;

☐ analyses of employees by age, sex, grade and length of service;

☐ time-keeping, absence and labour turnover statistics;

☐ records of total wages and salary costs.

Personnel records should contain only relevant information, and access to this information must be protected.

The Data Protection Act (1984) applies only to information held on computer files, but the principles are normally extended to paper-based systems in most organisations. The following principles were established by this Act:

1. The information contained on the record system must be obtained and processed lawfully. This means the purpose and use of various pieces of information must be made clear to the employee.

2. Data held by an organisation must only be used for the purpose specified on the Register, (since May 1986 all data users must register their systems with the Data Protection Registrar.)

3. The personal data held must be adequate, relevant and not excessive.

4. Personal data must be accurate and kept up-to-date.

5. Personal data must not be kept for longer than is necessary (there should be a policy regarding data held on employees who have left the organisation.)

6. Individuals are entitled to know what data is held about them, have access to it, and have the right to have the data corrected if it is found to be inaccurate.

7. Unauthorised access to data must be protected against.

3.6 Summary

In this chapter the essential elements of human resource planning have been covered. The process of assessing demand for labour and balancing it against supply has been outlined and statistical measurements have been introduced. The main features of the external labour market were outlined and you evaluated past, current and future trends. The job design and analysis process was explained and you assessed various formats for the job description. Finally, the administration systems needed to ensure an effective HR record system were described and the requirements of the Data Protection Act (1984) covered.

Further reading

Armstrong M, *A Handbook of Personnel Management Practice*, Kogan Page Ltd, Chapter 19

Bramham J, *Human Resource Planning*, IPM

Lewis D, *Essentials of Employment Law* (3rd edition) IPM, 1990, Chapter 17

Pearn M & Kandola R, *Job analysis a practical guide for managers* (2nd edition), IPM 1993

Ungerson B, *How to write a job description*, IPM 1990

Exercises

Progress questions

These questions have been designed to help you remember the key points in this chapter. The answers to the questions are on p125

Complete the following sentences:

1. Human resource planning is about...

2. Trend analysis assists demand forecasting by ....

3. The most significant demographic trends affecting the UK workforce are.................

4. Job design involves..

5. A job description would be called generic if it...

Select the correct response to the following statements:

6. The stability index includes data about staff who have been with the organisation for less than 1 year.

   True ☐ False ☐

7. Where demand for a particular category of employee is greater than supply, the organisation will need to encourage more applications.

   True ☐ False ☐

8. The proportion of people in the working population aged between 35-54 is predicted to increase each year between now and the year 2000.

    True ☐ False ☐

9. Having a large number of layers within the organisation's hierarchy increases the flexibility of the organisation.

    True ☐ False ☐

10. The Data Protection Act (1984) covers all forms of recorded information.

    True ☐ False ☐

Review questions

These questions have been designed to help you check your comprehension of the key points in this chapter. You may wish to look further than the text in this chapter in order to answer them fully. You will find your library useful as a source of wider reading. You can check the essential elements of your answers by referring to the appropriate section.

11. How can the future demand for labour within the organisation be estimated? (Section 3.4)

12. Outline some of the methods that can be used to carry out a job analysis. (Section 3.2)

13. What are some of the effects of technology on the labour market? (Section 3.3)

14. What sort of records may be kept on an individual employed by an organisation? (Section 3.5)

Multiple choice questions

The answers to these questions are given in the Lecturer's Supplement.

15. The measure that relates the number of leavers in the year to the average number of staff employed in the year is called:
    a) the stability index
    b) the cohort analysis
    c) the annual labour turnover index
    d) the half life analysis

16. Which of the following measures would help reduce the total supply of labour in the organisation?
    a) renewing fixed term contracts
    b) not replacing staff who leave
    c) speeding up training programmes
    d) transferring staff between departments

17. In which of the following sectors have most new jobs been created in the last 10 years?
    a) the manufacturing sector
    b) agriculture and mining
    c) the service sector

18. Participant observation involves:
    a) watching another person perform their job
    b) interviewing the job holder's colleagues
    c) undertaking the work tasks yourself
    d) completing a work diary

19. Which of the following principles was established by the Data Protection Act (1984)?
    a) personal data must be accurate, kept up-to-date and not kept for longer than is necessary
    b) all personal data held by the organisation must be registered with the Data Protection Registrar
    c) monitoring data on race, sex, marital status and disability must be kept

Practice questions

A marking guide to these questions is given in the Lecturer's Supplement.

20. Describe how organisations can adjust the balance of supply and demand for labour in the short-term HR plan.

21. How do effective HRM record systems assist the planning process?

22. How is the labour force predicted to change between now and the end of the century?

Questions for advanced students

A marking guide to these questions is given in the Lecturer's Supplement.

23. How could you evaluate the effectiveness of the HR planning process in the short and medium term?

24. For an organisation with which you are familiar, try to predict the effects that the increased use of new technology will have in the next 5 years.

Assignment: Planning for the future at Barnstone's Bookshops

A marking guide to this assignment is given in the Lecturer's Supplement.

Barnstone's Bookshops have been gradually expanding their retail outlets in order to develop and diversify the business. The corporate plan states that the company intends to purchase a similar size stationery company and merge the two businesses. Negotiations are currently taking place with the receivers of a bankrupt stationery chain and subject to a satisfactory agreement the merger will go ahead.

Barnstone's currently employ 200 staff in 25 locations, the stationery chain employs 180 staff in 18 locations. The jobs of the retail staff in the bookshops and stationers will be combined into a new multi-task post.

The 20 best retail sites will be identified and developed over the next year, with the remainder being closed down. This will result in a reduction of the new combined workforce by 50 staff overall.

Required

You are the HR director for Barnstone's, and are responsible for planning the future personnel requirements of the organisation.

i)   What further information will you need in order to construct your HR plan?

ii) How will you analyse the new job requirements for the combined bookshop/stationery posts?

iii) How will you implement the reduction of the workforce by 50 staff?

4 Employee resourcing

4.1 Introduction

This chapter looks at the way employees are appointed within the organisation to ensure the requirements of the HR plan are met. It begins by examining the analysis that takes place whenever a vacancy occurs and then develops into a consideration of the various recruitment methods. The analysis of the job requirements and the personal qualities of the individual are covered, as well as the techniques used to design an effective advertisement. The use of curriculum vitae and application forms is also included. The selection process is reviewed from the shortlisting stage through to final selection and the chapter concludes with a look at the employment contract which forms the basis of the employer/employee work relationship.

This chapter provides coverage of the "contribute to the recruitment and selection of personnel" unit of the MCI management NVQ.

On completing this chapter you should be able to:

❑ evaluate the possible courses of action to take whenever a vacancy occurs in the organisation and select the most appropriate;

❑ analyse the task and person requirements of a job in order to identify the key selection criteria;

❑ construct an effective advertisement and be able to identify suitable sources of recruitment;

❑ use the selection criteria to design an effective shortlisting system;

❑ evaluate the use of final selection methods such as interviews, aptitude tests, personality inventories and assessment centres;

❑ understand the basis of the contract of employment and discuss the use of employment references.

4.2 Recruitment processes

Before a recruitment decision can be made, the organisation must reflect upon any vacancy that occurs and link the decisions to the objectives set by the HR plan of the organisation. As we saw in section 3.2 the HR plan sets a strategy for resourcing the organisation and each individual vacancy will need to be linked to this strategy before deciding how to proceed. In some cases the organisation may be reducing staff overall, so the vacancy could provide the opportunity to transfer another employee from an over-staffed area. The promotion and succession plans may have prepared other employees to take on this job, so that there is movement at various levels within the organisation. The job as it stands, may need to be re-designed for future work needs, or the tasks may be divided up differently. Technology may be introduced or upgraded which could reduce the need for some elements of the job. All these factors need to be properly evaluated before the decision to recruit is finally taken.

An important step at this stage is to gain a thorough picture of the requirements of both the job and the individual, so that selection criteria can be drawn up. These criteria can then be used to determine if there is a suitable internal candidate and to identify any training needs they may have. In addition, these criteria can also be used for external recruitment.

As we saw in section 3.4, part of the HR planning process involves analysing jobs and preparing job descriptions that summarise key tasks. These job descriptions should be updated regularly, but a vacancy requires another thorough examination of the relevance of the current job description to the future needs of the post. From the current job description amendments should be made, and a concise summary gained of the essential job requirements in terms of tasks to be performed. For recruitment purposes, decisions then need to be made about the skills and experience needed by the individual who will take on this job. This person-based data is sometimes added to the job description to provide a single job specification document, or is produced as a separate person specification to be used in conjunction with the job description. Techniques of job description compilation were covered in section 3.4. For recruitment all that would be required is to up-date the tasks and remove any jargon or references to particular company systems. In the identification section, a fuller description of the context and nature of the organisation may be added if the company is not one well known to all applicants.

Activity

Write a brief paragraph describing the type, size and nature of the Marks & Spencer organisation for a foreign applicant not familiar with this company.

Marks and Spencer are a national chain of retail stores specialising in clothing, home furnishings and food products. There are .... stores throughout the U.K. and ..... stores on the continent. Marks & Spencer prides itself on its reputation for high quality both in the products sold and in service provided to customers.

When compiling the personal requirements of the job the same type of analysis is needed as for the job factors themselves. The qualities and experience of the existing job holder(s) may be reviewed, and any previous specifications examined. The judgement of the line manager would be sought as well as the advice of a personnel or HR specialist. The main factors under which the personal requirements are normally analysed are:

1. the previous work experience;

2. the aptitudes, special skills or competences;

3. the academic level;

4. the professional knowledge and qualifications;

5. the personality characteristics;

6. the personal requirements.

For selection purposes it is useful to distinguish between essential levels of each factor that must be possessed by the job applicant, and the desirable features that will be used to discriminate between those who meet the essential requirements at final selection stage.

Work experience

Essential previous work experience should define the minimum nature and length of work experience which a candidate should have in order to stand a realistic chance of fulfilling the demands of the job. Most candidates apply for jobs in order to further their careers and provide new challenges, so defining experience only in terms of exactly the same content and level as that on offer may be far too restricting. The ability to define experience that, whilst not being identical to the vacancy, should provide good evidence of the aptitude to succeed is the desired skill.

Aptitudes, skills and competences

When defining the essential aptitudes, skills and competences needed, a vast range of possibilities can be produced, for example:

- verbal fluency and communication skills
- writing ability
- analytical ability
- fluency with numbers/calculations
- language skills
- creativity
- computer skills
- typing/shorthand skills etc

What is important is to establish firstly, why the skill is needed ie what should the individual be able to do? and secondly, at what level the skill is needed. For recruitment purposes the organisation needs to consider realistically, what evidence is possible to collect in order to assess this skill requirement. It is all very well specifying "leadership skills" as essential, but how will evidence of leadership be deduced from an application form or c.v. at the shortlisting stage?

The practicalities of using the person specification details need to be thought through at each stage with particular emphasis on equal opportunities and the removal of unnecessary barriers to entry (see chapter 5).

The NVQ system provides one objective way of assessing various competences and the level of attainment.

Academic level

This factor attempts to define the minimum level of intellectual ability required in the job, which is often translated into particular academic qualifications as a convenient way of illustrating the level required. Stating the level required as GCSE Grade C or above does not necessarily mean that only those with this qualification will be considered, but it should mean that this is the level of ability required by the job itself. When shortlisting it may be possible to deduce from previous work experience that an individual possesses the ability to operate at this level even if they do not possess this actual qualification. Equivalent qualifications and NVQ units should also be considered.

There is a view in some organisations that a maximum level of intellectual ability should also be set as those over-qualified are unlikely to be stimulated by the job. The degree to which this is relevant would depend on whether the organisation is prepared to develop the job holder and prepare them for future vacancies at a higher level, or whether the strategy is simply to recruit those who are satisfied to stay where they are.

Professional knowledge and qualifications

This should state the minimum knowledge required to understand the particular subject matter of the work ie. financial services, engineering, computer programming etc. In some cases the level of knowledge can be expressed in terms of professional qualification using the same conventions as for academic ability. For example, the candidate should have passed the professional examinations of the IPD (Institute of Personnel and Development) or CIMA (Chartered Institute of Management Accountants) or an NVQ Level 4 in Financial Services etc. Once again the decision needs to be made as to whether this qualification is essential, or whether other evidence from short courses and work experience would be accepted as equivalent.

Personality characteristics

Personality characteristics are more deep-rooted than either skills or competences which can be acquired through experience or training. An adult's basic personality is not easily changed and it will largely determine the way in which the individual behaves at work. There are problems in specifying any factors in this area, however, as there is no single agreed definition of personality as a reference point. There is some evidence of a correlation between personality traits and some occupations, but this is usually no more than a broad trend and the danger is that to select on the basis of broad trends may be to select average rather than outstanding performers.

It is also easy to make assumptions about desirable personality characteristics based on the personality of the previous job-holder or based on unconscious stereotyping.

Unless the selection process is going to use sophisticated and well validated personality inventories, it is probable that all that can be attempted is a general description of a pattern of personality which on the basis of informed common sense appears desirable. This should not be used as essential criteria, however, to avoid excluding any candidate who may demonstrate suitability for the job by using other evidence. Those personality characteristics which would raise doubts about a candidate's suitability could also be identified so that they could be examined more closely.

Personal requirements

Personal requirements are those related to health and to personal or domestic situations. The relevance of the health of the individual to the job itself would depend on the nature of the work. Setting as essential, unnecessary levels of fitness and health will exclude those with disabilities of any kind. Some organisations require all short-listed candidates to have a medical examination. Others believe that provided a candidate can show no more than a normal pattern of sickness absence from employment references there is no need for a medical examination. Where medicals are required there should be a clear policy about what health conditions raise doubts about suitability and why.

Defining as essential various personal and domestic circumstances also provides scope for unfair discrimination and false assumptions to be made. It is far preferable that aspects of the job that may impact upon the candidate's willingness or ability to perform the job are clearly stated at the outset, so that they can consider carefully whether they wish to apply. Some examples could be:

❏ the job requires extensive travel within the U.K. and overnight stays approximately once each month;

❏ the job involves frequent presentations to clients so a firm, clear speaking voice and self confident manner is required.

Activity

Using these headings and the essential and desirable categories, devise a possible person specification for the job description of a secretary at level 1, illustrated in section 3.4.

Factor	Essential	Desirable
Work experience	Work placement or temporary job for 2–3 weeks in clerical or typing position in any type of organisation.	Longer placement or office junior experience.
Aptitudes, skills and competences	Communication skills: Verbal – confident and friendly verbal communication. Written – accurate, neat and well presented written work.	Some evidence of the ability to organise and prioritise work to show aptitude to develop to level 2 secretary.
Intellectual level	GCSE English grade C or above (or equivalent).	4–5 GCSE passes in a range of subjects at grade C or above.
Professional knowledge and qualifications	Typing skills at RSA Level II (or equivalent). Wordprocessing qualification and knowledge of WordPerfect 5.1. Shorthand at 50 wpm.	Studying for RSA Level III and higher WP and shorthand levels.
Personality characteristics	Friendly, positive personality showing self confidence and the ability to take direction and seek help when necessary.	Keen to learn and develop skills further.
Personal factors	Good, clear speaking voice for telephone calls and direct customer contact. Occasional requirement to travel to provide support at regional conferences (2–3 times per year).	

Once the job analysis and person specification details have been prepared the next decision is how to publicise the vacancy to suitable applicants.

Activity

Consider the following sources of recruitment:

1. for what type of jobs would they be most suitable?;
2. state whether they would be a high, medium or low cost method for the organisation to use.

- internal job advertisements
- advertisement in a local newspaper
- advertisement in a professional journal
- advertisement in the national press
- notice in shop window
- advertisement in the Job Centre
- note to the school's career service
- visit to school/university careers fair
- using a commercial employment agency
- contacting a selection consultant
- word of mouth, or employee contacts
- reviewing speculative job applications received.

The use of internal job advertisements would probably be part of the recruitment policy of the organisation for vacancies at all levels to ensure existing employees have access to promotion or job changes. For one-off, fairly junior, locally based jobs the most suitable additional sources of recruitment would be:

- advertisement in a local newspaper
- notice in shop window
- word of mouth, or employee contacts
- advertisement in the Job Centre
- reviewing previous or speculative job applications received.

The low-cost methods include the informal methods such as word-of-mouth, and using a notice in a shop window, but the number of respondents will be very restricted and the organisation may be found to be indirectly discriminating (see chapter 5). Reviewing previous or speculative applications has no cost and may be productive if school leavers are required, but the best applicants will probably already have found other positions, so this would only be worthwhile if the applications have been received recently. Advertising in the Job Centre has no cost and could attract a newly unemployed suitable candidate who would be available to start work immediately. There may not be a suitable candidate if the skills or knowledge requirement is higher, however. Medium cost options include advertising in the local press. The choice of publication will depend on the job itself and the readership of particular publications.

Visits to schools/universities and advertisements placed with the careers service would be useful if the job was suitable for a school/university leaver, and the vacancy occurred at the end of the academic year. Recruitment by these methods would normally only be cost effective if there are several vacancies to fill, however.

For more specialist or senior managerial jobs the following sources would be suitable in addition to internal recruitment:

☐ advertisement in a professional journal

☐ advertisement in the national press

☐ using a commercial employment agency

☐ contacting a selection consultant

Internal recruitment may still be an important source of applicants for specialist and managerial jobs, particularly if the organisation has invested in employee development. In some cases the essential skills are not available however, and the national or even the international labour markets need to be accessed. Advertisements in professional journals would be cost-effective if the job was based in one functional area. There is often a range of possible publications, so research would be needed into the likely readership and response rate for each. For a more generalist post, national press advertising may be an alternative using a paper that is recognised as a source in the field. The costs of this are extremely high, however, and there will be a lot of wastage. For this reason, commercial employment agencies may be used who place the advert for the client and ensure that a shortlist of candidates is available. The agency will charge a significant fee for this facility, however, and the quality of the service will need to be monitored carefully. Selection consultants can also provide specialist help with recruitment and may already have suitable candidates on their books.

If a decision is made to use an advertisement, the organisation will then have to decide whether to use the specialist services of an advertising or recruitment agency, or produce the advertisement "in house". This decision is dependent on the skills available within the organisation on drafting an effective advertisement, and the seniority or importance of the vacant post.

The main points to consider when writing an advertisement are:

☐ *the general image;* which should attract the reader's attention, be appropriate to the type of job on offer, and convey the organisation's corporate style. The use of corporate logos is a frequently used device.

☐ *the information to include;* this should cover the job, the organisation, the selection criteria, the salary and benefits and how to respond. Job and person details should be extracted from the job analysis documents. Salary ranges should be specified, and the key benefits highlighted, and the applicant should be clearly aware of what is required to progress the application. Is more information available, and if so how should it be obtained? Are curriculum vitae's or application forms to be used? Is there a closing date? Candidates should be invited to reply to named individuals rather than anonymous PO box numbers.

☐ *the style and emphasis;* the job title, location and salary are the main features sought by potential applicants so these should be immediately identified and highlighted. The use of borders and variety of type styles and sizes adds interest but should not be too fussy. Bullet shots or lists may help organise key points. In more expensive advertisements the use of illustrations or photographs may be incorporated. Humour or catchy slogans can also be used if appropriate.

❑ *the detailed text*; the ability to summarise key aspects of the job and write cost-effective text is a vital skill. Cliches and technical jargon should be avoided. The text should follow a logical sequence and cover all necessary details. The text must also ensure that equal opportunities requirements are fulfilled (see section 5).

Activity

Compile an advertisement to be placed in the local press for the Secretary's job at level 1, based on the job description and person specification produced before (sections 3.4 and 4.2).

The organisation is the Thrifty Insurance Company, the job is located in central Manchester, and the salary range is £9,000-£12,000 per annum with private health insurance and staff discounts on insurance products.

An example of the type of advertisement that could be produced is shown below:

SECRETARY

THRIFTY INSURANCE COMPANY

MANCHESTER

The Company: Thrifty Insurance Company is a successful direct mail insurance company offering a wide range of motor and personal insurance products.

The job: We require a secretary to carry out, under supervision, typing and wordprocessing assignments to support a team of 4–5 sales staff. Shorthand and audio-typing are required, as well as diary management, filing, and receptionist duties.

The candidate: The ideal candidate will have a good grade GCSE pass in English, possess typing skills at RSA level II (or equivalent) and shorthand at 50 wpm. A knowledge of wordprocessing, preferable WordPerfect 5.1 is also essential. Previous work experience in a junior clerical or work placement position is required, and good interpersonal communication skills.

The benefits: a salary of £9,000–£12,000 depending on experience is offered, with full private health insurance and staff discounts on other insurance products.

Please write to Mrs . . . . . . for an application form and further details at the following address:

Thrifty Insurance Company
Manchester M . . . . . .

The closing date for applications is . . . .

THRIFTY INSURANCE COMPANY IS AN EQUAL OPPORTUNITIES EMPLOYER

(Applications are welcomed from all sections of the community, but particularly from those who are disabled, or a member of an ethnic minority group who are under-represented in our workforce.)

Obviously, the style and layout will vary depending on personal preferences, but this kind of detail and structure provides a model.

4.3 Selection methods

The content of the job advertisement provides the first selection device. If the advertisement has been written carefully it will exclude the unsuitable candidates leaving a smaller field to shortlist.

The organisation will have decided by this stage whether to collect data from candidates by curriculum vitae or application form.

Activity

Consider what the advantages and disadvantages may be for the organisation and the applicant in using either a c.v. or an application form.

For the organisation, application forms allow data to be collected in a standardised format allowing easier comparisons. An effectively designed application form can be structured around the shortlisting criteria and questions can be selected to extract the most relevant information. The disadvantages may be the difficulty of having standard forms that meet all the recruitment needs of the organisation, and the missed opportunity to see the candidates own individual style of presentation. For the candidate the advantage of the application form is that the required data is clearly evident, but some forms may be difficult or time-consuming to complete which may discourage a good applicant.

Curriculum vitae's are more individual, allowing the candidate more flexibility in what they choose to include. They can be difficult to compare, however, and some necessary data could be missing. C.V.'s are normally more suitable for individual, fairly key posts, whereas application forms are more useful for routine recruitment exercises.

When conducting any selection activity it is essential that individual bias is minimised as far as possible. The most effective ways of doing this are:

1. to establish objective selection criteria before the selection process begins which will be applied to all candidates;

2. using two or more individuals in the selection process to minimise any unfairness caused by personal bias.

At the shortlisting stage the selection criteria must be able to be assessed from the c.v./application form. The criteria should be derived from the person specification but could also include factors such as the quality of presentation of the c.v. and/or covering letter. Various assessment systems can be produced to assist the process. For example, a list of essential criteria could be produced with a YES/NO response against each. Shortlisting would use this checklist and be based on the number of YES answers completed. Difficulties arise if the criteria used are not so clear cut, so some organisations may use a rating scale ie:

Excellent 1 2 3 4 5 6 Not present

It may also be necessary to apply a weighting factor to each criteria if some are considered more important than others. For example, a YES to some questions would be worth x2 or x3 the value of a YES to another question.

It is important that all those involved in shortlisting are assessing the criteria in the same way. One way to double-check this is for two assessors to rate the applications independently, and then compare their assessments. If there are great disparities the selection criteria may need to be refined further.

Shortlisting aims to reduce the total number of candidates down to a manageable number for final selection. For each vacancy 4-6 final selection candidates would be adequate in most cases. One factor in deciding the size of the final selection cohort will be the methods of final selection that are being used. If group assessment is part of the process then larger numbers may be required. During the shortlisting stage it is vital that all applicants are kept informed by letter, of the progress of their application. Control lists should be made for each vacancy which log the applicants then chart what happens to the application. Those applicants rejected at the shortlisting stage must be written to and told their application was unsuccessful. Those invited for final selection should be sent the details for the next stage, and a few applicants may be put on hold in case they are needed later. If there is likely to be a delay between the closing date and shortlisting a postcard confirming the application has been received and telling the candidate a further letter will be sent shortly, is useful.

The main final selection techniques are:

❑ interviews
❑ psychometric tests and personality questionnaires
❑ presentations/demonstrations
❑ group selection methods
❑ references

The choice of technique(s) depends on the nature of the vacancy, the selection criteria used, and the investment the organisation is prepared to make in the process. Interviews and references are the most frequently used selection methods, but further supporting impressions may be sought from other methods.

As with shortlisting the final selection criteria should be established in advance, and an acceptable assessment system designed. The selection method(s) used must be reliable ie produce the same results if used more than once, and valid ie measure the factor they set out to measure.

A brief outline of each technique will be given below:

Interviews

Selection interviews take many different forms from brief 10 minute chats to lengthy structured sessions. The interview has been demonstrated to have limitations as a reliable predictor of future job performance, but it can be significantly improved by having a properly structured approach, and by using trained interviewers.

The problems associated with interviews are linked to the personal bias of the selector mentioned before. Interviewers have a frame of reference based on their own value judgements and life experiences. Candidates with similar views to the interviewer may be preferred over those from different backgrounds. Interviewers may stereotype the type of person needed for the post. If the job has always been filled by a woman the interviewer may consciously or unconsciously stereotype the work to the disadvantage of male applicants. Studies also show that physically attractive people are treated more favourably than those who are less attractive. The first and last impressions made by a candidate may be weighed particularly heavily, and may lead to a halo or horns effect. The halo effect occurs when a good first impression leads the interviewer to focus on all the positive aspects of the interview, discounting unfavourable details. The horns effect works in the opposite direction with a negative first impression leading to the interviewer seeking out reasons not to employ the candidate.

Language itself may provide a barrier to communication, hesitant or jargon filled conversation is less well received than well expressed ideas. Non-verbal communication or body language may also convey a message to the interviewer. For example, a candidate who slouches in the seat, or who will not make eye contact, may appear uninterested or furtive.

Obviously in some cases the way the candidate performs at interview may be directly relevant to their ability to do the job. In other cases, however, a good interview technique may mislead the interviewer into attributing the candidate with more job competence than they possess. Conversely, an able candidate with poorer interview technique may not be appointed for the wrong reasons.

Training in how to structure and progress the interview can help minimise these problems and assist a more objective selection. Having more than one interviewer also minimises personal bias. Interviews can be conducted in tandem (using two interviewers), in sequence (with individual interviews taking place one after the other) or using a panel (3 or more interviewers). In all these cases there will be more than one viewpoint obtained which should minimise the effects of personal bias.

Interviews remain an important selection technique because they are ideal for collecting more information about the candidate to supplement the application form or c.v. details. They also allow the interviewer to give the candidate more details about the job and for the candidate to ask questions of the interviewer. A face-to-face meeting allows the interpersonal and verbal communication skills of the interviewee to be assessed.

Activity

Imagine you are preparing to conduct an interview for the Secretary post outlined before, what would you need to do before the interview to ensure you are properly organised, what would you need to do during the interview to appear professional, and what would you need to do after the interview has finished?

Before the interview a reasonable amount of notice should be given to allow candidates to make the necessary arrangements. Where practicable, there should be flexibility for the candidate to request a more convenient date. Adequate information must be provided about the length of the interview, the staff involved in interviewing, test procedures where applicable and details of how to get to the location. The company policy on payment of expenses for attending interviews must be clearly stated to candidates in the invitation letter prior to attendance at the interview. The location chosen should be quiet and free from interruptions, and the layout of the room conducive to a friendly discussion. Interviewers should be fully conversant with the job and person specifications and the criteria established for selection. Questions should be prepared to obtain the information for assessment against the job criteria.

During the interview a professional approach should be taken which involves:

❏ structuring the interview with an introduction which welcomes the candidate, introduces the interviewers, and sets out the plan of the interview. This should be followed by questions about the candidate and information about the job. The candidate should have the opportunity to ask questions, and the interview should be formally concluded, ensuring that all parties are clear about the next step;

❏ asking a range of different types of questions ie open-ended questions to allow information to be gathered, probing questions to gain additional details, and follow-up questions to check understanding of what has been said. Closed questions that can be answered by yes or no should be used with care, and leading questions (that indicate to the candidate the correct answer) and multiple questions avoided. Questions should be asked consistently to all the candidates interviewed for a specific vacancy, and discriminatory questions avoided.

❏ taking notes on the information obtained either during or immediately after each interview to aid the memory when carrying out the final assessments;

❏ keeping to the time allocated to the interview.

After each interview, the candidate should be assessed against the selection criteria independently by each interviewer. At the end of the session all candidate assessments should be compared and a decision taken on whether an appointment is to be made, or whether further selection efforts are needed.

Psychometric tests and personality questionnaires

There are many different types of test designed for different purposes. A basic distinction is normally made between tests of performance ie mental ability tests and measures of personality ie personality questionnaires. Both tests and questionnaires should be objective, standardised measures; they require a highly controlled, uniform procedure for administration and scoring. For every candidate the test items and instructions should be the same; the time allowed should be the same if it's a timed test and the physical test conditions should be the same. For tests of ability the items should be organised so that the easier items appear first to allow the candidate to settle into the test. The difficulty level of the question is normally established at the design stage by calculating the percentage of those taking the tests who got the item correct.

Psychometric tests and questionnaires are usually objectively scored. The administrator has a key which contains the right answers for a test, or the value to be given to a specific answer on a multiple-choice questionnaire. Therefore, with objectively scored tests the scorer's judgement does not lead to variations in score, and many tests today are computer-scored.

Another factor which determines objectivity and standardisation is the way in which the score is interpreted. The number of items correct on an ability test, or the sum of values for responses on a questionnaire scale, constitutes the raw score. This is then compared with the range of scores obtained from a large representative sample of people for whom the test was designed. The sample may be drawn from the general population or from more specific groups such as UK graduates, or craft apprentices. The results provide norms which relate all scores to the distribution around the average established from the sample group. It is important that precise information is given about the way these norms are drawn up so that a valid test is selected.

Many organisations have designed psychometric tests and questionnaires, it is important when choosing a measure that it is a reputable one, that it is supplied with instructions for administration, scoring and interpretation, including norms, and the details of its reliability and validity are obtained.

There are several different types of psychometric test, the main ones are:

❏ attainment tests;

❏ general intelligence or aptitude tests;

- ❑ special aptitude tests;
- ❑ trainability tests;
- ❑ personality assessments.

Attainment tests are designed to measure the degree of knowledge and/or skill a person has acquired at a particular point in time. Academic examinations are one type of such a test. Attainment tests include tests of numeracy and literacy, and tests of practical skills such as typing or shorthand.

General intelligence or aptitude tests are designed to provide a measure of the individual's capacity to learn or to perform a task in the future, irrespective or present training and experience. In practice, however, it is extremely difficult to design a test that does not rely at all on previous experience or education. Designing tests of intelligence is also problematic because there is no one agreed definition of what intelligence is. Most general intelligence tests aim to examine a range of different abilities together with the speed of problem solving. The simplest form of general intelligence test would be a mixture of verbal (ability with words and meanings), numerical (ability with numbers) and spatial (ability with pictures or diagrams) items. Higher level tests such as those of abstract reasoning may also be used.

Special aptitude tests concentrate on one type of ability rather than providing a more general picture. Tests are designed to measure specific job aptitudes such as verbal ability, or numerical ability, manual dexterity, or mechanical ability. Other special aptitude tests are based around specific jobs such as word processor aptitude, or computer programming aptitude.

Trainability tests are purely practical. They involve asking an applicant to perform a specific, job-related task in which he or she has been given prior instruction. By noting the number of errors made and the way in which the applicant approaches the task, judgements can be made about the potential of the individual to do the job and respond to training.

Personality assessment is problematic because there is no one agreed definition of personality. Different theorists have put forward ideas about how personality is formed, and how it can be described. The two main ideas which have been linked to personality questionnaires are:

- ❑ type theories, which classify personality by a series of choices between alternative types of behaviour, for example extravert/introvert, or passive/active etc ;

- ❑ trait theories, which measure personality factors against a rating scale to show the degree to which the individual possesses this factor. The number of traits used in these measures may vary, but by plotting the results on each scale a profile can be formed of the individual's unique personality.

Once the method of assessing personality has been established questionnaires can be constructed that allow these factors to be measured by plotting the answers to particular questions. Personality questionnaires tend to be quite lengthy and ask the same sorts of question in a variety of ways. The candidate's responses are assessed against the norms and a picture of their personality characteristics can be formed. These questionnaires require careful analysis and those administering them will need training to ensure they are being interpreted correctly. Often a narrative description of personality factors may be produced to support the profile.

It is important with any kind of psychometric measure that the evidence produced is used in a balanced way. Test results can be improved by practice and familiarity with the format, and nerves or tiredness may interfere with the results gained. Ideally, each candidate should have the opportunity to sit a test on two or more occasions, and an average of the results taken. With personality assessments candidates may answer the questions in the way that they think the employer will favour rather than from their true values. The use of objective situations or questions that have equally favourable choices can help to eliminate this. Some tests also have lie scales to pick up candidates who are answering inconsistently or in an unrealistic way.

Presentations/demonstrations

Where a job requires particular skills the selection procedure may include a demonstration of the skill to a panel of observers/selectors.

Activity

What type of job task or skill could be assessed in this way?

There are many alternatives available, but the ability to make a formal presentation is one example of a managerial skill that could be assessed by this method. The candidate should be briefed beforehand on the type and length of the presentation required. The observers who watch it need to be trained in what to look for, and how to evaluate performance. Assessment forms incorporating rating scales may be designed for this purpose. Other forms of demonstration could include setting up simulations of real activites and asking the candidate to respond to them. Case studies, in-basket exercises, or role-plays could be used to assess other managerial skills. Care is needed when using these methods that the evidence produced is reliable and valid, however.

Group selection methods

Group methods assess the interaction between candidates in a group situation in order to evaluate leadership, team work and interpersonal skills. The ways of doing this are similar to those of the previous section, through exercises, role-plays and simulations. Group discussions and leaderless group tasks can also be used to examine the roles that individuals take in such activities. Once again the observers need to be trained to record their observations and evaluate them effectively.

References

Most employers include the taking up of references as part of their selection procedure. References may be requested before or after the selection decision is made. In either case the candidates express permission should be obtained before a referee is approached. If references are used as part of the selection process the referees of all shortlisted candidates will need to be obtained before the appointment is made. References can then be used together with all the other final selection techniques when deciding which candidate to appoint.

Other employers prefer to take up references only after the candidate has been selected. In this case references are only used to confirm basic factual details given by the candidate. It is common for letters of appointment in this situation to include the phrase "subject to satisfactory references".

Information provided in a reference is often given in confidence, but if included in a computerised record system the provisions of the Data Protection Act (1984) could be used by an employee to gain access to this data. Most previous employers will be quite happy to confirm factual details, but may be more reluctant to give information about the candidate's suitability for the job applied for, or to answer more general personality questions.

References from previous employers normally provide the most valid data, character references from friends are obviously far less objective. Some organisations follow up written references with telephone calls. The information obtained verbally may be more candid, but care should be taken in case a biased or ill informed viewpoint is obtained.

Overall the two vital questions that should be asked of any previous employers are:

1. Would you re-employ this individual?

2. Do you know of any reason why we should not employ him/her?

As well as employment references, in some cases organisations may ask for medical references following a medical examination or the completion of a medical questionnaire. Under the Access to Medical Reports Act 1988 the candidate must give their permission before their G.P. is contacted, and indicate whether they wish to see the report produced.

Having now looked at the various selection methods individually, it is clear that the effort put into final selection can vary enormously according to company policy. Where the selection is for a key post or when individuals with high potential are sought, various selection techniques may be combined together into an *assessment centre*. The assessment centre would use multiple methods of selection to provide the most valid assessment of the candidate possible. A combination of interviews, tests and group activities are normally arranged over a 1-2 day period. Candidates may also be assessed informally during meals and coffee breaks etc. The validity of properly organised assessment centres is high compared with other methods used individually. The costs of running such exercises are also high, however, so the cost-effectiveness needs to be judged carefully.

4.4 *The employment contract*

Once a decision to appoint a candidate has been made, an offer of employment must be made either verbally or in letter form. The candidate may then accept or reject the offer made. The contract of employment results from this oral or written offer and acceptance, together with "consideration" which means reciprocal promises or obligations made by both parties. In this case the employer promises to pay the employee in return for the employee's promise to work. The terms of the contract may be both express (written down) and implied (understood informally by both parties).

Under the Employment Protection (Consolidation) Act 1978 as amended by the Trade Union Reform and Employment Rights Act 1993, an employer must give the employee a written statement setting out particulars of his/her employment not later than 2 months after the employment commenced.

This statement must specify:

❐ the names of the employer and the employee;

❐ the date when the employment (and any period of continuous employment) began;

- remuneration methods and intervals of payment;

- hours of work;

- holiday entitlement;

- sickness entitlement;

- pensions and pension schemes;

- notice entitlement;

- job title or a brief job description;

- where it is not permanent, the period for which the employment is expected to continue or, if it is for a fixed term, the date when it is to end;

- either the place of work or, if the employee is required or allowed to work in more than one location, an indication of this and of the employer's address;

- details of the existence of any relevant collective agreements which directly affect the terms and conditions of the employee's employment – including, where the employer is not a party, the persons by whom they were made.

Additional details must be provided for employees who are expected to work abroad regarding the period of employment abroad, the currency in which the employee is to be paid, any additional pay or benefits and terms relating to the employee's return to the U.K.

The statement must also include details of the employer's disciplinary (except in firms with fewer than 20 employees) and grievance procedures or a reference to where they can be found. It should also state whether or not a pensions contracting-out certificate is in force for the employment in question.

The written statement may refer to another reasonably accessible document for particulars of pension schemes, sickness entitlement, disciplinary rules and appeals procedures.

All employees working for 8 hours a week or more (except in firms with fewer than 20 employees) , are also entitled to an itemised pay statement which must include details of gross pay, net pay, variable deductions (with detailed amounts and reasons) and fixed deductions.

4.5 Summary

In this chapter the essential elements of employee resourcing have been covered. The chapter began by examining how vacancies are reviewed and how effective job descriptions and person specifications are compiled. Sources of recruitment were analysed and the procedure for writing an effective job advertisement was covered. Techniques of short-listing were then described, followed by a review of the final selection techniques of interviews, psychometric tests and personality questionnaires, presentations/demonstrations, group selection methods and references. Assessment centres were described and the chapter ended with a review of the terms of the employment contract itself.

Further reading

Aikin Olga, (1993) *Contracts – Law and Employment Series*, IPD

Fraser J M, (1958) *A Handbook of Employment Interviewing*, London, MacDonald & Evans

Herriot P, *Recruitment in the 90's*, IPD

Lewis C (1985) *Employee Selection*, London, Hutchinson

Lopez F M (1975) *Personnel Interviewing* (2nd ed) Maidenhead, McGraw Hill

Plumbley P, *Recruiting for Profit* (5th ed), IPD

Toplis J, Dulewicz V & Fletcher C, *Psychological Testing: A Manager's Guide*, IPD

Torrington D, Hall L, Haylor I & Myers J, *Employee Resourcing* (Management Studies 2) IPD

Woodruffe C, *Assessment Centres – identifying and developing competence*, IPD

Exercises

Progress questions

These questions have been designed to help you remember the key points in this chapter. The answer to the questions are on p125

Complete the following sentences:

1. A person specification is ....

2. The 3 most important details looked for in a job advertisement are ....,

   .... and ....

3. Bias in interviewing can be minimised by ....

4. Special aptitude tests are ....

5. The validity of a selection technique is...

Select the correct response to the following statements:

6. Job centres do not charge the employer for advertising a vacancy.

   True ☐ False ☐

7. Advertisements should include a salary or salary range to indicate the approximate remuneration for the job.

   True ☐ False ☐

8. Leading questions are a useful device to get the interviewee talking.

   True ☐ False ☐

9. Aptitude tests measure the candidate's current degree of knowledge or level of skill.

   True ☐ False ☐

10. The contract of employment is a written statement of the terms and conditions issued to the employee.

    True ☐ False ☐

Review questions

These questions have been designed to help you check your comprehension of the key points in this chapter. You may wish to look further than the text in this chapter in order to answer them fully. You will find your library useful as a source of wider reading. You can check the essential elements of your answers by referring to the appropriate section.

11. How should the job and person requirements of a post be analysed before any recruitment and selection process begins? (Section 4.2)

12. Describe how to construct an effective shortlisting system. (Section 4.3)

13. What are the main advantages and disadvantages of the interview as a selection method? (Section 4.3)

14. What are the main types of psychometric test? (Section 4.3)

15. Outline the essential details that must be contained in a written statement of terms and conditions of employment. (Section 4.4)

Multiple choice questions

The answers to these questions are given in the Lecturer's Supplement.

16. Which of the following sources of recruitment would be cost-effective for a junior position:
    a) national advertising
    b) executive search agency
    c) job centre
    d) professional journals

17. General intelligence or aptitude tests:
    a) measure specific job aptitudes
    b) measure the degree of knowledge and/or skill a person has acquired
    c) measure the individual's capacity to learn or perform a task in the future

18. The contract of employment is formed by:
    a) the written statement of terms and conditions of employment
    b) the letter offering the candidate the job
    c) the offer and acceptance of a job based on an agreement to exchange work for payment

19. The person specification should include:
    a) details of the pay and holiday entitlements of the post
    b) the job tasks to be performed
    c) the knowledge and experience of the candidate
    d) details of the company location and activities

Practice questions

A marking guide to these questions is given in the Lecturer's Supplement.

20. Describe the main features of an effective recruitment advertisement.

21. Outline the main steps that should be taken to ensure a reliable and valid selection interview is carried out.

22. What contribution can psychometric tests and personality questionnaires make to the selection procedure?

Questions for advanced students

A marking guide to these questions is given in the Lecturer's Supplement.

23. Outline a programme of group assessment activities which would help to select management trainees for an organisation, stating why you included each item.

24. Select some recruitment advertisements from the national press, local press and technical journals/professional magazines. Compare and contrast the style, content and layout of the advertisements in each.

Assignment: Recruiting management trainees at Mollusc petro-chemicals

A marking guide to this assignment is given in the Lecturer's Supplement.

Mollusc petro-chemicals is a major multi-national employer in the oil and chemical industry. Each year graduate trainees are sought in various functional areas.

You are the newly appointed graduate recruitment manager at Mollusc, and have been asked to put together a programme to recruit and select management trainees to specialise in Human Resource Management within the U.K. operations.

Required

i) Outline the sources of recruitment you intend to use, and comment on the style and layout of any advertisements that would be produced.

ii) State how you would compile your shortlist for final selection, and outline the content of the final selection programme.

iii) Produce a model written statement of terms and conditions of employment for these recruits.

5 Equalising employment opportunities

5.1 Introduction

This chapter looks at how organisations can develop policies and procedures that maximise the opportunities available to all employees and prospective employees in the workplace and ensure equality of treatment for all. It begins by looking at the legal framework to support equal opportunities and reviews case law, it then assesses the effectiveness of the legalistic approach. Issues affecting sex equality and gender discrimination are reviewed, followed by a consideration of racial equality. The employment of the disabled is the third focus area and the chapter ends with a look at age discrimination.

This chapter provides the underpinning knowledge for many of the competence requirements identified in the MCI standards.

On completing this chapter you should be able to:

❏ describe the main legal statutes affecting equal opportunities;

❏ compile equal opportunities policy statements and devise procedures to enforce them;

❏ assess the main factors affecting sex, race and disability discrimination and outline ways of overcoming them;

❏ explain how equal opportunities monitoring and positive discrimination programmes assist in re-balancing the workforce.

5.2 The legal requirements

The term discrimination, when used in relation to employment, means favouring one individual in preference to another. This is not necessarily a negative process; as we saw in the previous chapter most selection procedures involve discriminating in favour of the best candidate for the job. The aim of equal opportunities legislation is to ensure that discrimination in employment is not made on an unfair or unlawful basis on the grounds of sex, marital status or race.

The main U.K. legislation covering sex discriminations is:

❏ the Sex Discrimination Act (1975) as amended in 1986
❏ the Equal Pay Act (1970) and the Equal Pay (Amendment) Regulations 1983
❏ the Employment Act (1989)
❏ the Social Security Act (1989)
❏ the Trade Union Reform and Employment Rights Act (1993)

The Sex Discrimination Act (1975) established 2 forms of discrimination:

1. *Direct* discrimination: where a person is treated less favourably than another person is (or would be) treated because of his/her sex or marital status;

2. *Indirect* discrimination: where a requirement or condition of work is (or would be) applied equally to both men and women (or married and unmarried) but has a disproportionate detrimental effect on one sex (ie that the proportion of women within the group who can comply is significantly less than the proportion of men).

Activity

Which of the following examples shows direct discrimination, and which shows indirect discrimination?

a) The candidate must be under 5 foot 4 inches tall.

b) Waiter required for high street restaurant.

c) Applicants must have worked continuously for 10 years and have an unbroken track record of successful selling.

d) The ideal candidate will be single, mobile and enthusiastic.

In these examples b and d are directly discriminating. In b the term waiter indicates that a male applicant only is required. The advertisement should either specify waiter/waitress required, or be re-worded so that the job content is described (applicants are required to wait on customers ....). In d it is unlawful to specify that the candidate must be single. Examples of indirect discrimination may result from a and c if the requirements are not essential for the job. Setting a height restriction of 5 feet 4 inches will disadvantage male applicants, so this will be unlawful unless the employer can prove that the job can only be performed by small people (which seems unlikely). Similarly the restrictions in c may disadvantage women applicants if they have taken a career break to raise a family.

The Sex Discrimination Act (1975) made it unlawful to discriminate against either women or men in the following employment areas:

❏ recruitment and selection arrangements (including advertising)

❏ the terms on which jobs are offered

❏ opportunities for training, transfer or promotion

❏ access to any facilities, benefits or services

❏ dismissal (including redundancy)

The Sex Discrimination Act (1986) also removed the discrimination between the sexes in respect of the age of compulsory retirement.

There are a limited number of jobs for which it is possible to specify either a male or a female is required. Section 7 of the Sex Discrimination Act 1975 establishes the following main areas of genuine occupational qualifications (G.O.Q's) these are:

❏ jobs requiring authentic male or female characteristics such as acting or modelling;

❏ jobs where privacy and decency require that they are provided by a person of the same sex;

❏ jobs where there is single sex accommodation only and it would be unreasonable to expect the employer to provide extra accommodation for both sexes;

❏ jobs in single sex institutions such as hospitals or prisons;

❏ jobs where welfare, education or personal services are best provided by a person of the same sex;

❏ jobs which involve travel to a country where the laws and customs prohibit males or females;

❏ jobs that are advertised as one of two to be held by a married couple.

Activity

Analyse the following situation and decide whether the job does contain a genuine occupational qualification:

Miss Wylie applied for a job as a shop assistant at Dee & Co (Menswear) Ltd. The manageress refused to consider her for the position because she felt the job was unsuitable for women on the ground that assistants sometimes had to take the inside leg measurements of male customers. The manageress claimed that the job was a GOQ because a man was needed to ensure privacy and decency.

This example was based on a real case (Miss S Wylie v Dee & Co (Menswear) Ltd, Glasgow IT: Case No. S/4161/77). The decision made was as follows:

The job did not need to be done by a man to preserve decency and privacy because the need to take inside leg measurements of male customers did not arise frequently in the job. Cubicles were provided for customers to try on garments, and other methods of obtaining the measurements could always be used (for example measuring a customer's own trousers while he tried on a new pair, or asking one of the 7 male assistants to help).

In addition to the Sex Discrimination Acts, the Equal Pay Act (1970) and the Equal Pay (Amendment) Regulations 1983 cover discrimination between women and men in respect of pay and other terms and conditions of employment. It establishes the right for women (or men) to receive the same pay and conditions where they are involved in like work, work rated as equivalent or work of equal value. When defending an equal pay case the employer must show that any differences in pay are based on either differences in the content of the jobs (differences of practical importance) or differences in the qualifications, skills or experience that the individuals bring to the job (material differences).

Activity

Consider the following two cases, do you think the claim for equal pay was successful, and was the decision based on the differences in the job performed, or on the differences between the personal qualities of the individuals?

a) A female relief clerk/typist claimed equal pay with a male clerk as they were performing broadly similar work.

b) A woman cleaner sought equal pay with a male labourer/driver. Both did cleaning and tea-making but the man spent 18% of his time on driving.

In both cases the equal pay claim failed, in a) because there was a material difference between the two based on the fact that the woman was a stand-in and did not have the experience or job knowledge of the regular employee. In b) the case failed because it was judged that the extra driving duties constituted a difference of practical importance.

The U.K.'s involvement with the European Community means that the law must also comply with Articles 118 and 119 of the Treaty of Rome, the Equal Pay Directive (1975) and the Equal Treatment Directives (1976) and (1986). These re-inforce the principles of equal pay for equal work, and provide for equality in social security (provided by both the State and the employer), state benefits (except pensions) and company benefits (except pensions). The U.K. enforced these requirements in the Social Security Act (1989) where both direct and indirect discrimination was made unlawful in respect of pensions and other termination of employment benefits. Finally, the Trade Union Reform and Employment Rights Act 1993, legislated against discriminatory terms in collective agreements and rules of employment.

Legislation in the area of racial discrimination is covered by the Race Relations Act 1976. The Race Relations Act 1976 covers discrimination on the grounds of colour, race, nationality or ethnic or national origins. The Act does not expressly prohibit discrimination on religious grounds but it has been held that certain religious groups, including Jews and Sikhs, constitute racial groups because of their ethnic origins.

European law does not specifically prohibit racial discrimination but Article 48 of the Treaty of Rome requires that any discrimination between workers of Member States based on nationality in relation to employment, remuneration and other conditions of work, should be abolished.

The Race Relations Act 1976 was drafted very similarly to the Sex Discrimination Act 1975, and again incorporates the concepts of direct and indirect discrimination.

Activity

Consider whether the employer carried out unlawful racial discrimination in the following case:

> An employer refused to appoint a black female minicab driver on the grounds that she could be subject to racial attacks in that area.

This was a real case (Ace Mini Cars Ltd and Long v Albertine, EAT 18.10.90, 262/89) and the judgement was that this was a case of direct racial discrimination.

There are a limited number of genuine occupational qualifications listed in the Race Relations Act, these include:

❑ jobs which require a person from a particular racial group for reasons of authenticity, for example in acting, modelling or being a waiter/waitress in an ethnic restaurant;

❑ jobs which provide a community service for a particular ethnic group.

Individuals who wish to bring a case under either the Sex Discrimination Acts, the Equal Pay Acts or the Race Relations Act, should bring the matter to the attention of the employer concerned in the first instance. If the employer denies the claim the case may be taken to an Industrial Tribunal (see section 8.5) within a 6 month period. The

Industrial Tribunal will then give a judgement on what further action or compensation is necessary.

The Sex Discrimination Act 1975 set up the Equal Opportunities Commission (E.O.C.) to promote equality, carry out investigations, conduct research and issue guidelines and codes of practice. Similarly the Race Relations Act 1987 set up the Commission for Racial Equality (C.R.E.) with the same remit in the area of race discrimination.

Other pieces of legislation designed to promote equality of opportunity include:

❏ the Disabled Persons (Employment) Act 1944 as amended by the 1958 Act;

❏ the Rehabilitation of Offenders Act 1974

The Disabled Persons (Employment) Act established a register of disabled people. Disablement resettlement officers issue certificates of registration which disabled people can show to employers when seeking work. The 1944 Act set a quota of 3% registered disabled in the workforce for employers of 20 people or more. It is not a legal offence to have fewer, but technically employers should not recruit able-bodied people without a permit to do so. There are few, if any, prosecutions under the Act, however. The 1958 Act reserves certain occupations expressly for disabled people e.g. lift and car park attendants. Recently, additions to the existing rights of the disabled have been proposed in the Civil Rights (Disabled People) Bill, but no new legislation has yet resulted.

The Rehabilitation of Offenders Act 1974 was designed to assist offenders when seeking employment by setting rehabilitation periods after which a criminal offence would be "spent" (not have to be declared). The rehabilitation period varies from 5 years to life depending on the seriousness of the offence and the length of the sentence imposed. Some offences are never spent. The Act does not apply to jobs in the health and social services, teachers, accountants and police. Employers who discover an applicant has a spent conviction and refuse to employ the individual do not commit an offence themselves, nor are they liable to compensate the applicant.

Overall the role of legislation in increasing equal opportunities in employment is debatable. The legislation has certainly resulted in far less direct discrimination, jobs are no longer advertised just for men or women (unless a GOQ), but indirect discrimination is much less easy to eradicate. In the area of equal pay, differentials between male and female earnings are still significant. The equal pay legislation has also been criticised for being complex and time-consuming to implement. Some significant case law has evolved in the area of discrimination, however, which has established certain precedents and set out what is expected from good practice in employment.

5.3 Sex equality

Some of the facts that indicate the existence of sex discrimination in the U.K. are:

❏ the vast majority of women employees are in low paid occupations in the service, retail and health sectors

❏ 40% of the total workforce are women but only 4% of middle and senior managers are female

❏ 80% of all part time work is performed by women

❏ women's average pay rates are two thirds that of men

The factors that have contributed to this situation are historical, economic and social in origin. Historically women have been seen primarily as homemakers rather than being part of the paid workforce. The traditional role of women was as housekeepers and childrearers, supporting their male spouses who went out to paid work. When women did perform paid work they were concentrated in the caring professions such as nursing, social work or education, or into low grade office/manual work such as typing, assembly or machining. It was common for women to be paid a lower rate than their male colleagues simply because they were female. Women were also expected to withdraw from the labour force when they married, the civil service operated a marriage bar for many years. During the 1st and 2nd world wars women were drafted into the labour force to replace male workers at war. After the 1st world war women gave up these jobs and returned to the home, but after the 2nd world war women were more reluctant to leave the workplace. Women have been referred to as "the reserve army of labour" to be called upon in times of shortage but then released again if the male employment situation changes. There are many people today who argue these historical values still affect attitudes to employment today.

As seen in the previous section, legislative and social changes have caused a significant alteration in the status of women in employment today. Direct and indirect sex and marriage discrimination is now unlawful, and employers must provide equality of opportunity for both sexes. Recent changes to maternity leave provision (see section 8.5) may mean that employers are more wary than ever of employing women, however.

The Equal Opportunities Commission recommends that the first step that must be taken by any employer is to formulate a written equal opportunities policy.

Activity

Outline what you think an equal opportunities policy should contain.

The Equal Opportunities Commission has published a model which many employers have adapted to their own needs. Most policies will include the following:

a) a definition of direct and indirect sex and marriage discrimination, victimisation and sexual harassment;

b) a statement of the organisation's commitment to equal opportunities;

c) the name/s of the officer(s) responsible for policy;

d) details of structure for implementing the policy;

e) an obligation upon employees to respect and act in accordance with the policy;

f) procedures for dealing with complaints of discrimination;

g) examples of unlawful practices;

h) details of monitoring and review procedures;

i) a commitment to remove barriers to equal opportunity.

In order to implement this policy the EOC recommends that a senior manager at the highest possible level should be given overall responsibility for equal opportunities. The policy should be written and distributed widely, and training provided on its implementation. An equal opportunities committee or working party should be set up to implement the policy and review and evaluate its progress. Monitoring should also take place to measure the number of male/female and married/single applicants for vacancies and the progression of male and female employees through the organisation. Monitoring is normally done by asking applicants to complete a monitoring form as well as the application form and then returning it to a monitoring unit. Monitoring data should be kept completely separate from that used for selection. Analysis of appointments and applicants could then indicate if, and where, discrimination is occurring.

The main areas where sex discrimination could be found are:

❐ in recruitment, particularly when compiling the person specification and the job advertisement;

❐ in the questions asked on an application form;

❐ in the selection criteria adopted;

❐ in questions asked at interview;

❐ in tests used for selection;

❐ in the use of references;

❐ in access to promotion opportunities;

❐ in access to training and development;

❐ in the value attached to jobs and the method of pay;

❐ in the hours of work and employment conditions.

Activity

How could you prevent unfair sex discrimination occurring at each of the stages described above?

In recruitment and selection, as well as monitoring all applicants, the characteristics on the person specification should be examined to ensure they are not discriminatory. Stereotyped assumptions about women's disposition or personal circumstances should be avoided, so should age restrictions or mobility requirements which may indirectly discriminate against women. Requiring current work experience will also disadvantage women returning after a career break, so consideration should be given to other forms of relevant experience, including unpaid work. The application form itself should not include questions about marital status, numbers and ages of children, spouses employment etc. Data needed for personnel records can be obtained after employment, and the monitoring form can be used to check employment practices. Advertisements must not use single sex words to describe the job (salesgirl etc) and care should be taken not to use illustrations that suggest one particular sex would be more suitable.

Selection criteria should not include stereotypical or biased criteria, for example "this is a dirty job so it's not suitable for a woman". At the interview the questions asked should be posed to all candidates both men and women.

Activity

Consider whether the following questions are discriminatory:

a) what arrangements would you have to look after your son if you had to work at short notice?

b) do you intend to have children in the future?

c) how do you feel about working in an all female environment?

In all cases these questions are discriminatory, and particularly so if not asked of all applicants both male and female. Questions about specific job requirements should be phrased neutrally, for example in a) above the question could be re-worded – you will occasionally be required to work until 7.00 pm at rather short notice, would you be able to do this?

Hypothetical questions about future intentions such as b) are both impertinent and irrelevant, no candidate either male or female can accurately predict their future circumstances. Question c) is also likely to be construed as discriminatory by any male applicants.

Tests used for selection need to be carefully checked to ensure they don't favour either males or females. Details of the norm population used to validate the test should be examined to ensure a proper balance of men and women was used. Monitoring should also take place to see whether the tests eliminate more applicants of one sex than the other.

The requirement to have up to date employment references may discriminate against women returning to the labour force after a career break. Alternative types of referee should be accepted, maybe from unpaid employment positions.

Access to promotion requires many of the same safeguards as initial selection. Where promotion requires the recommendation of a line manager, monitoring should take place to ensure the individual is not ignoring or passing over certain candidates. Promotion based on length of service or seniority may also disadvantage those with career breaks, and should not be used as the sole factor for selection.

Regarding access to training and development, details should be kept on the numbers of men and women, single and married, who receive training and the type of training received. The employer should check that women are expected and encouraged to undertake training as fully as men, that they receive the same on the job training and that existing training programmes do not reflect different career expectations for men and women.

In pay and terms and conditions of employment, organisations should check all terms and conditions by reference to sex and marital status. Differential rates of pay between men and women must be justifiable on grounds other than sex, and job evaluation schemes, bonus schemes and merit payments must be free from sex bias. Part time staff should receive the same pro rata terms and conditions as full time employees if they perform similar work.

Where the organisation discovers evidence of past discrimination Sections 47 and 48 of the Sex Discrimination Act 1975 allows employers to take certain forms of remedial action (also known as positive action or affirmative action). Employers are allowed to encourage one sex to train for, or apply for, certain jobs (women into engineering or men into nursing). It does not allow the employer to discriminate by sex when it comes to selecting who will be recruited or promoted, however. It is also not lawful to try to correct an imbalance by operating a quota system.

A final issue in sex discrimination is that of sexual harassment. The E.C. Recommendation 1991 (Protection of the dignity of women and men at work) states that Member States should take action to promote awareness that conduct of a sexual nature, or other conduct based on sex, is unacceptable if:

a) such conduct is unwarranted, unreasonable and offensive to the recipient;

b) a person's rejection of, or submission to, such conduct is used explicitly or implicitly as a basis for a decision which affects that person's access to vocational training, access to employment, continued employment, promotion, salary or any other employment decisions;

c) such conduct creates an intimidating, hostile or humiliating work environment for the recipient.

The I.P.D. statement on harassment at work makes the following points:

❏ It is necessary to distinguish sexual harassment from, for example, sexual relationships freely entered into and acceptable to those involved. (Although the conduct of sexual relations at the workplace during working time may, in itself, be a disciplinary matter).

❏ It is not the intention of the perpetrator but the deed itself and the impact on the recipient which determines what constitutes harassment.

Activity

List the ways in which sexual harassment could take place, giving examples of the kinds of behaviour that would be unacceptable.

Forms of harassment may include:

a. physical assault (ranging from touching to serious assault);

b. verbal and/or written harassment (jokes, offensive language, gossip etc);

c. visual display (posters, graffiti, obscene gestures etc);

d. coercion (pressure for sexual favours);

e. intrusion (pestering, spying, following).

❏ Employers are liable for the actions of their employees in the course of employment – whether or not the employer knows of the employee's action.

As stated in the previous section, although some advances have been made by using legislation, much more remains to be done and equality of opportunity is still dependent on initiatives undertaken voluntarily by organisations rather than required by the state. A recent example of such an initiative was Opportunity 2000 launched with government backing in 1991 in order to improve the position of women in the labour market. Under the auspices of this scheme organisations are introducing initiatives which will allow women to combine careers with other commitments, but the initiatives that have been adopted tend to be relatively low cost solutions such as flexible working, career breaks and extended maternity leave rather than the more costly benefits like workplace nurseries.

5.4 Racial equality

Some of the facts that indicate the existence of race discrimination in the U.K. are:

❑ one in four black workers and one in five Asians were out of work in 1993, with figures in certain inner-city areas exceeding 40% for each group;

❑ in 1991 members of ethnic minority groups were twice as likely to be unemployed as members of the white population;

❑ ethnic minority workers are significantly more likely to be long-term unemployed (unemployed for over 6 months);

❑ people from ethnic minority groups are more likely to be found in semi-skilled and unskilled work even when levels of qualifications are taken into account.

The factors that have contributed to this situation are partly historical, based on patterns of immigration, and partly social and economic. After the 2nd World War the U.K. experienced a labour shortage, particularly in low grade manual jobs. Active measures were taken to encourage immigrants from the Commonwealth countries to come to the U.K. This resulted in a significant influx of ethnic workers to the urban manufacturing areas of the midlands, London and the north. Immigrant workers were housed in low grade accommodation, often in the city centre, and undertook the manual jobs white U.K. workers no longer wanted. Fairly rapidly concern was expressed about this policy and the government introduced a series of progressively more restrictive Immigration Acts to reduce the inflow. Some British workers felt strongly that jobs were being "stolen" from them and racism became more prevalent and unpleasant. Today, of a total workforce of around 28 million, 4.6% are from black or Asian origins, and of these over half were born in the U.K. and three quarters are British citizens.

Workers from ethnic minority groups are more likely to be in low status occupations in the retail, health and hotel and catering sectors. Like women, ethnic workers appear to form a "reserve army of labour" called upon in times of labour shortage, but vulnerable to redundancy in times of over supply. As a result more ethnic workers choose to become self-employed (particularly in the Asian community). There is also a very low rate of penetration of ethnic workers in white collar occupations.

The Commission for Racial Equality (C.R.E.) was set up by the Race Relations Act 1976 to help to address this situation. Like the Equal Opportunities Commission the first recommendation is that an organisation should incorporate within its equal opportunities policy, measures to ensure the equal opportunity for all workers from different ethnic backgrounds. The CRE's Code of Practice to ensure effective action recommends the following steps:

1. The allocation of responsibility to a senior executive for racial equality issues;

2. Consultation with the workforce, trade unions and outside bodies on race equality;

3. A statement of policy should be written down and publicised widely;

4. Training in equal opportunities issues should be provided;

5. All existing procedures and criteria should be examined to ensure they provide equality of opportunity to all races;

6. Monitoring should include details of the ethnic backgrounds of all applicants and employees;

7. Positive action should be taken to redress any existing imbalance in the ethnic grouping within the workforce.

A CRE investigation in 1994 of the 168 largest companies in Britain showed that 88% had a stated commitment to racial equality in their employment practices. However, only 45% of the companies had implemented or were about to implement an action plan or programme. For this reason the CRE launched a new standard for racial equality in January 1995 called Racial Equality Means Business to help employers move from "words to deeds". The standard aims to translate the CRE's Code of Practice into action. There are 3 main areas to the standard:

1. The case for action – the argument that there is a close relationship between running a business well and implementing fair employment practices.

2. A checklist that summarises the range of actions that may be involved in considering, planning and implementing a racial equality programme.

3. The largest section of the standard covers measures of progress. These measures are the key to the whole approach, outlining five levels of achievement across six broad areas; policy and planning; selecting, developing and retaining staff; communication and corporate image; corporate citizenship; and auditing for racial equality.

Organisations should ensure that all existing procedures and criteria are examined for possible discriminatory practices. As with sex discrimination, recruitment and selection procedures should be particularly closely examined to ensure no direct or indirect discrimination occurs. Monitoring data on the ethnic origin of all applicants should be collected.

Activity

Design a monitoring form to collect details of the applicant's ethnic origin.

The example shown below complies with the CRE's guidelines:

Application for the post of . . . .

Vacancy Reference Number . . . .

1. I would describe my cultural and ethnic origin as:
   (indicate by placing an X in appropriate box)

African		Chinese	
Asian		Cypriot	
Caribbean		Irish	
UK European		Other European	

Any other (please specify) . . . .

Selection criteria should be examined to see if essential academic qualification discriminate against applicants educated in another country. The criteria set for a job should not include levels of written or spoken English that are not consistent with the job content.

Any tests used should be examined to see if they are "culture fair" (they contain items that can be equally well answered by all nationalities). Records should also be kept to see if more ethnic minority applicants are eliminated by a test than white applicants.

At the interview stage, deliberate or unintended racial discrimination by interviewers must be eliminated, and individuals who show hostility to those from different ethnic origins counselled or disciplined. Questions about an ethnic minority applicant's ability to "fit in" with white colleagues should be avoided as well as undue questioning on dietary requirements or holiday time needed for religious observance. These questions all imply a discriminatory attitude.

Training can also considerably help understanding of race equality issues and create a more sympathetic attitude. Some employers have incorporated modules on equal opportunity into existing company training programmes, such as induction training, recruitment and selection training, management training etc. Others have established specialised training and briefing programmes on equal opportunities. Topics covered in equal opportunity training have included:

❑ an examination of the nature of discrimination intentional and unintentional and how it occurs;

❑ the relevant legislation provisions and their implications;

❑ briefing on the cultural background of minority group workers;

❑ reviewing the mechanics of the equal opportunities programme and its practical implications.

The provision of business language courses for employees whose communication skills disadvantage them for promotion could also be considered.

The Race Relations Act 1976 also provides for positive action to be used to redress an imbalance within the workforce. They do not allow the imposition of quotas or permit discrimination in selection.

Activity

How could a positive action programme encourage more applicants from ethnic backgrounds?

Among the measures that have been implemented are:

☐ job advertisements designed specifically to reach members of ethnic minority groups under-represented in the workforce and to encourage applicants from such groups;

☐ recruitment and training schemes for school leavers designed to reach members of under-represented groups and to meet any special training needs;

☐ encouragement to employees from such groups to apply for promotion and training for promotion;

☐ skill training for employees who lack particular expertise but show potential.

Finally, the organisation needs to consider how instances of racial harassment will be dealt with within the organisation. Racially motivated attacks, taunts or victimisation should be dealt with severely using the organisation's disciplinary procedures (see section 8.6)

5.5 Employment of the disabled

The quota system introduced by the 1944 Disabled Persons (Employment) Act has been described as "ineffective, outdated and unenforceable" (D.O.E. 1990). The stigma attached to the disability registration scheme also means that there are substantial numbers of disabled people not on the register. In April 1989 the total number of disabled people registered was 366,768 but the Labour Force Survey in Spring 1989 identified 1.85 million people of working age in employment who had health problems or disabilities which limited the type of work they could do (6.6% of the working population).

Those with work limiting health problems or disabilities have very high unemployment rates (18% according to the 1989 Labour Force Survey). Over 22% of these had academic or vocational qualifications at A levels or above. Disabled adults in employment have also been found to earn significantly less than the working population in general, even when hours of work are taken into consideration.

The poor employment prospects for disabled people led to the drafting of the Civil Rights (Disabled Persons) Bill which was put before parliament in May 1994. This bill was "talked out" at that time, but the Conservative government have made a commitment to providing an alternative piece of legislation to assist the disabled. Proposals include giving disabled people the right to take an employer to an Industrial Tribunal if they are unfairly discriminated against when applying for a job, and making it a legal requirement that all new buildings are designed so that disabled people can use them.

Currently there is a Code of Practice for people with disabilities and organisations are encouraged to make more opportunities available for disabled people in the workplace.

Activity

Activity

Outline the main ways that an organisation can help to provide equal opportunities for disabled people?

Firstly, the organisation should have a commitment not to stereotype disability. Disabilities are wide ranging in their nature (eg lack of mobility, visual impairment, hearing, learning difficulties, speech, epilepsy, diabetes) and are not confined to any particular group or section of the community. Disability is not always life-long and permanent, some individuals become disabled later in life, and others are only temporarily disabled as a result of accident or illness.

Secondly, the organisation should not unduly restrict the occupations for which disabled people are suitable. Technology advances have made many more jobs possible for those with disabilities, and grants and advice are available to employers who need to adapt the workplace to suit a disabled employee.

Thirdly, organisations should monitor applicants and employment opportunities available to disabled candidates.

Finally, organisations should carry out any positive discrimination activities necessary to help redress an existing imbalance in the workforce.

Activity

How could a positive action programme encourage more disabled applicants?

Positive action could take place by offering training and placements to disabled individuals. Recruitment advertising could be targeted towards the disabled by using non-written media such as local radio, or making direct links with training centres for the disabled. More part-time or supported employment opportunities could be provided. Some organisations also guarantee that all disabled candidates that meet the basic essential criteria for the job will be interviewed.

5.6 Age discrimination

There is no legislation in the U.K. that expressly prohibits discrimination on the basis of age. Age discrimination can affect many people, however, particularly older workers, the young and women returners. It consistently favours those in the 25-35 age group.

Many people over the age of 55 are already economically inactive (not working or seeking work). The gap in activity rates between those under and over 55 has widened sharply since the early 1980's. It has been claimed that the older worker is the main victim of the recession because employers are relying on early retirement, and voluntary redundancies (involving many older workers) to cut the workforce.

Many older workers would still like paid work, one study found that a quarter of people aged 50-70 would like to return to work. The labour market itself is changing with an increasing number of people in the over 40's age group. One estimate suggests that by the year 2000 one in three people in the labour force will be aged over 40. This is coupled with a decrease in the number of young people entering the labour force. As a result, employers may well be forced to re-examine the assumptions they are making about older employees.

Activity

What are the assumptions that are often made about older people as employees?

The main assumptions, that can result in some very misleading stereotyping, are:

❏ effective job performance is directly linked to age;

❏ physical and mental ability is directly linked to age;

❏ older people are less adaptable and less receptive to training;

❏ absenteeism is worse for older people.

Studies have disproved all these assumptions, there is no general link between the factors, each individual should be judged on his/her own merits not by age.

As with other forms of discrimination, the employer should examine existing employment practices to see if they disadvantage older workers, monitor applicants and employees to see if there is unfair discrimination against particular age groups, and consider positive action initiatives to increase the proportion of people in under-represented age groups.

The I.P.D. provide the following recommendations for eliminating age discrimination:

Recruitment and Selection:

❏ advertising

The use of age, age related criteria or age ranges in job advertisements is not recommended unless clearly identified as positive action to attract more individuals from an under-represented age group. It is important not to use age in job advertisements to exclude people in particular age groups. The purpose of job advertisements is to attract the best qualified candidates for satisfactory job performance. It does not make good business sense to deliberately exclude suitably qualified candidates on the basis of age.

❏ application forms

It is desirable to state that age criteria will not be taken into account in employment decisions. It should be used for monitoring purposes only.

❏ the selection interview

Interviewers and those concerned with selection decisions must be aware that subjective, stereotypical views about age are dangerous, as is judging an individual's age on the basis of physical characteristics or appearance.

Medical Advice

An individual's age should not be used in order to make judgements about their physical abilities or mental fitness. Where such a judgement is required, an occupational health or medical practitioner should be consulted.

Remuneration

Pay and terms and conditions of employment should not be based on age or age related criteria but should reflect the degree to which an individual meets the required standards of satisfactory job performance and the value of their contribution to the overall objectives of the organisation.

Training and Development

It is inefficient to automatically exclude people in particular age groups from training and development programmes.

Reorganisation, Retention and Redundancy

The future needs of an organisation regarding particular knowledge, skills and competencies should be taken into account when decisions about the retention and redundancy of individual employees are made. Both long and short term implications should be considered.

It is important to remember that older workers tend not to change jobs as frequently as young employees and correspondingly offer good potential return in employment and training investment.

Alternatives to redundancy such as shorter hours, part-time working, contractual arrangements etc should be considered.

Retirement

The issue of pensions and retirement age is an important one in many organisations. Research indicates that many older workers would welcome an opportunity for phased retirement and more flexible working.

5.7 Summary

In this chapter the essential elements of Equal Opportunities have been covered. The chapter began with a review of the main legislation from both the U.K. and the E.C. in this area, and then went on to look in more detail at sex equality, race equality, disability and age discrimination. The section on sex equality reviewed the historical changes in ideas about men's and women's work, and identified some facts that illustrate the continuance of sex discrimination in employment today. The content of an Equal Opportunities Policy is reviewed and ways to prevent unfair sex discrimination are covered. The section on race equality looked at the facts that indicate race discrimination exists in the U.K. and reviews measures taken by the Commission for Racial Equality to promote the necessary changes in employment practices. The section on the employment of the disabled looks at the ineffectiveness of the current legislation and outlines the main ways organisations can help provide opportunities for disabled people. The chapter ends with a look at age discrimination in employment.

Further reading

Birkett K & Woman D, *Getting on with disabilities: An Employer's Guide*, IPD

Clarke L (1993) *Discrimination*, IPD

C.R.E. *Implementing Equal Employment Opportunities*

Positive Action & Equal Opportunity in Employment

Why keep ethnic records? – Questions and answers for Employers and Employees

Indirect discrimination in Employment: A Practical Guide

Code of Practice: For the elimination of Racial Discrimination and the Promotion of Equality of Opportunity in Employment

E.O.C. *Guidelines for Equal Opportunities Employers*

Fair and Efficient Selection

Avoiding sex bias in selection testing

Positive action and Recruitment Advertising

Job evaluation schemes free of sex bias.

HMSO *Code of Practice on Equal Opportunities*

Code of Practice on the Employment of the Disabled.

IPD Research Series: *Age and Employment: policies, attitudes and practice.*

Exercises

Progress questions

These questions have been designed to help you remember the key points in this chapter. The answer to the questions are on p126

Complete the following sentences:

1. Direct discrimination is..

2. Genuine occupational qualifications are...

3. The main Act covering racial discrimination is ....

4. Positive action programmes are ....

5. The main ethnic groupings to be included on a monitoring form are........................

Select the correct response to the following statements:

6. Stating all candidates must have a beard is a form of indirect sex discrimination.

    True ☐ False ☐

7. It is illegal to include age criteria in a person specification.

    True ☐ False ☐

8. An advertisement that asked for an Asian community worker would not be illegal if the job requirements were a genuine occupational qualification.

True ☐ False ☐

9. Under the equal pay legislation only identical jobs can be used for comparison purposes.

True ☐ False ☐

10. The Disabled Persons (Employment) Act 1944 set a quota of 6% for the number of disabled people in the workforce.

True ☐ False ☐

Review questions

These questions have been designed to help you check your comprehension of the key points in this chapter. You may wish to look further than the text in this chapter in order to answer them fully. You will find your library useful as a source of wider reading. You can check the essential elements of your answers by referring to the appropriate section.

11. Explain the terms 'a difference of practical importance' and 'a material difference' as used in the equal pay legislation? (Section 5.2)

12. What are the genuine occupational qualifications under the Sex Discrimination Act 1975? (Section 5.2)

13. Outline the main ways in which sexual harassment occur. (Section 5.3)

14. What could an employer do to attract more people from under-represented age groups into employment? (Section 5.6)

15. What measures need to be taken to ensure selection tests do not discriminate on sex or racial grounds? (Section 5.3 and 5.4)

Multiple choice questions

The answers to these questions are given in the Lecturer's Supplement.

16. The Sex Discrimination Act was made law in:
    a) 1970
    b) 1975
    c) 1976
    d) 1983

17. Approximately what proportion of the total workforce of the U.K. in 1994 were women:
    a) 20%
    b) 30%
    c) 40%
    d) 50%

18. Which of the following questions asked at interview may be considered unlawful:
    a) how long have you worked for your current employer?
    b) could you work occasional weekends?

c) do you intend to start a family soon?

d) how old are you?

19. A positive action programme cannot:

a) promote a vacancy to redress an imbalance in the workforce

b) provide training to help individuals from an under-represented group

c) guarantee an interview for all applicants from an under-represented group that meet the basic essential criteria

d) impose a quota on the employment of people from specific ethnic groups.

Practice questions

A marking guide to these questions is given in the Lecturer's Supplement.

20 Outline the main issues that need to be examined in order to decide whether an equal pay claim is valid.

21. Describe the measures that need to be taken to ensure equal opportunities in recruitment and selection.

22. What is the purpose of equal opportunities monitoring, and how should the relevant data be collected?

Questions for advanced students

A marking guide to these questions is given in the Lecturer's Supplement.

23. Outline the content of an Equal Opportunities training course for newly appointed managers.

24. Review the advertisement for a Secretary at Thrifty Insurance Company in section 4.2 and suggest how it could be altered to more specifically target disabled people.

Assignment: Assisting equal opportunities at the T.E.C.

A marking guide to this assignment is given in the Lecturer's Supplement.

You are the equal opportunities advisor at your local Training and Enterprise Council (T.E.C.). You have been asked to prepare some aids for local employers to help them fulfil their responsibilities.

Required

i) Prepare a checklist of matters to consider when reviewing equal opportunities in the following areas:

☐ recruitment and selection

☐ induction

☐ training and development

☐ promotion

☐ pay and terms & conditions of employment

ii) Prepare a model equal opportunities monitoring form to be sent to all candidates with the application form, and give briefing notes on how the data should be used.

6 *Employee development*

6.1 Introduction

This chapter looks at the methods that can be used to help train and develop employees and constantly renew their skills. The term training is used to describe any activity that develops knowledge or skills in relation to a specific job or occupation. Development is used to describe a broader range of activities related more to the needs of the individual and their future careers. Obviously, the distinction between the two can become blurred, as many training activities can also be described as developmental.

The chapter begins by discussing how people can be encouraged to learn and then looks at the national framework for training and development in the U.K. The cycle of identifying training and development needs, designing and implementing programmes, and evaluating their success, is reviewed for the individual, the work group and the organisation as a whole.

This chapter provides coverage of the NVQ management unit "developing teams, individuals and self to enhance performance".

On completing this chapter you should be able to:

❑ discuss theories of learning and relate them to the needs of individuals, and particular training and development methods;

❑ understand the current U.K. framework for vocational education and training and describe the NVQ system;

❑ evaluate a variety of approaches to performance appraisal and be able to plan for an appraisal interview;

❑ be able to carry out a training needs analysis and design an appropriate programme;

❑ give feedback on a training/development event and understand the evaluation process.

6.2 Learning theories

One of the most fundamental skills a human being possesses is the ability to learn. Learning helps us make sense of the world around us and helps us acquire greater knowledge which in turn allows us to modify and develop our behaviour. The actual method by which learning occurs and the way our memory operates to organise ideas, thoughts and experiences is not widely understood. Different theories of learning are reflected in the design and implementation of different training and development events.

A few of the main theories and their training and development implications are outlined below:

1. One of the most readily accepted theories of learning is that individuals respond to feedback, and that behaviour will be modified if it is either rewarded (positive feedback) or punished (negative feedback). This approach is referred to as the behaviourist approach. Trainees need to be given feedback in order to refine and develop their skills and abilities.

Activity

Your new puppy needs to learn to be house trained. How could you reinforce the desired behaviour:

i)   by using positive feedback?

ii) by using negative feedback?

Positive feedback would involve showing the dog a suitable place, in the garden or on a litter tray, to perform its toilet and then giving great praise if the desired result occurred. Negative feedback would involve being angry and punishing the dog for any accidents.

It is only a small step to transfer such methods to a child, and the concept of positive and negative feedback is used in many adult learning situations. In day-to-day life most people learn what is acceptable behaviour by the way others react to them, this form of feedback is sometimes called conditioning. The rules and procedures of the organisation and the actual work tasks to be performed can all be learned via feedback and conditioning. Feedback is also a key element of performance appraisal (see 6.4).

2. A different set of ideas about learning, often referred to as the cognitive approach, states that human beings do not just learn by reacting to the stimulus provided by others, they also have a capacity for independent action which operates at a higher level than that of stimulus-response. The way an individual chooses between a variety of alternatives, the ability to plan ahead, and the basic curiosity of humans are all components of the cognitive system. Following on from this approach, training and development needs to challenge and interest the learner to be effective. The learner needs to gain satisfaction from the event. This relates back to the ideas about motivation which were covered in chapter 2.4.

3. In the area of memory and the retention of knowledge, theorists have concentrated on how individuals store and retrieve information in the brain. Memory is believed to operate at two levels, short-term and long-term and the method of storing information is crucial to knowledge retention and learning.

Activity

When revising for an examination what methods could you use to help store and reinforce the information you require?

Most people need to reinforce the storage of information by repeating and practising the material. The more times you repeat an activity the more deeply it is stored. You can also help code information by using key words or letters (mnemonics) or linking ideas to visual images. Having a context for learning also helps so that you have some background for the details you are trying to remember.

These principles are also important for many other learning activities, not just examinations. Putting the learning in context, and reinforcing by practise are important training and development techniques.

4. Another influential set of ideas about learning emphasise the importance of learning from experience (learning by doing). Experiential learning can be achieved from both positive and negative incidents. Various models of experiential learning describe the process as a cycle which involves firstly feeling (experiencing), then observing what has happened (reflection), then thinking through the implications (forming abstract concepts and generalisations), and then experimenting by trying out the modified behaviour (applying principles). The new experience then starts the cycle again and the skills and abilities are refined and developed further. Learning does not result simply from experiences, however, the active process of consideration and hypothesis formulation is essential to its success.

Activity

Many workplace activities involve constant experiential learning for skill development. As an example, when learning to use a keyboard on a computer or word-processor the operator needs to develop a range of skills to develop speed and accuracy. Consider how the process could be divided into the 4 stages described above:

1. Feeling/experiencing
2. Observation/reflection
3. Thinking (forming abstract concepts)
4. Doing (applying the principles)

At stage 1 the learner inputs some data using the keyboard. Stage 2 involves reflecting upon the result which could either be positive (an accurate piece of work) or negative (mistakes). At stage 3 the learner thinks about the reasons for the mistakes, for example the incorrect placing of the fingers, failure to use the space bar or enter key correctly etc and then modifies his or her behaviour accordingly. The final stage involves re-doing the work to see whether the analysis of the cause of the errors was accurate. The whole cycle would then begin again with further refinements of technique being made.

6.3 National frameworks and competence assessment

Before we look at in-organisational training and development it is important that the U.K. context of education and vocational support is understood. The education system has many objectives and these include preparing individuals for their role in society and their roles at work. Everyone receives education until the age of 16 in the U.K. and a National Curriculum attempts to ensure that all school leavers have at least a basic range of knowledge and skills. More recent initiatives, have included the introduction of more vocational, skills-based qualifications alongside the more familiar academic ones. During the 1990's a belief that knowledge was not the only desired outcome of education led to a more practical method of assessment based on what the individual can do. This system is known as the NVQ system which stands for

National Vocational Qualification, and can be acquired through full-time study at schools and colleges (GNVQ – General National Vocational Qualification) or through your employment.

NVQ's are divided into 5 levels of competence starting from a very basic level 1 up to the most advanced level 5. Each level is subdivided into units of competence, each of which are further subdivided into elements with accompanying performance criteria and range statements, see the diagram below.

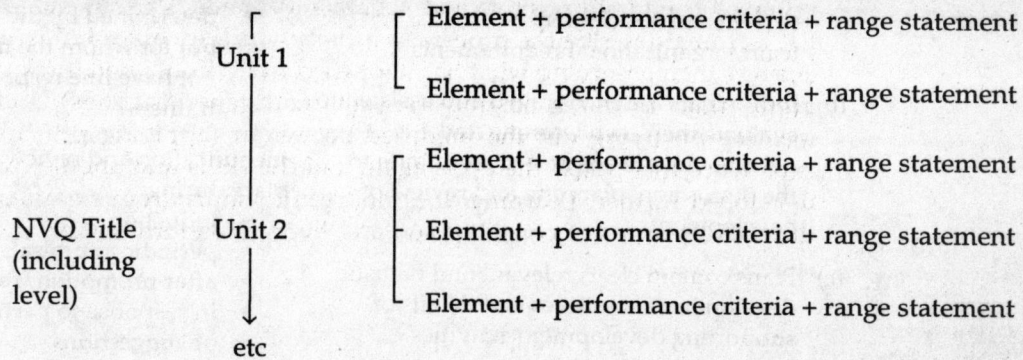

```
                    ┌        ┌  Element + performance criteria + range statement
            Unit 1  │        │
                    └        └  Element + performance criteria + range statement

                             ┌  Element + performance criteria + range statement
NVQ Title   Unit 2  │        ├  Element + performance criteria + range statement
(including          │        │
level)              ▼        └  Element + performance criteria + range statement
                    etc
```

A unit represents a discrete aspect of competence which can be certified independently. Elements are descriptions of something an individual should be able to do within an occupational area. They should specify an activity, the object of the activity and the conditions of the activity, and be capable of demonstration and assessment. Performance criteria are descriptions of the standards of performance required for the successful achievement of an element of competence. They should be expressed in terms of outcome. Range statements specify the range of applications of an element and its associated performance criteria in terms of activity, context, processes and equipment.

An illustration of the use of this framework is shown by the extract below taken from the Management I Occupational standards (NVQ level 4) devised by the Management Charter Initiative (M.C.I.) The Occupational Standards at this level contain 9 units, the example is from Unit 5:

UNIT   ELEMENTS

                                    ┌ 5.1   Develop and improve teams
                                    │   through planning and activities
Unit 1:5   Develop teams,   │
            individuals and self to ┤ 5.2   Identify, review and improve
            enhance performance   │   development activities for
                                    │   individuals
                                    │
                                    └ 5.3   Develop oneself within the
                                             job role

The performance criteria and range statements for Element 5.2 are shown overleaf:

Element I 5.2   Identify, review and improve development activities for individuals

Performance Criteria:

(a) Development objectives are based on a balanced assessment of current competence, potential future competence and career aspirations and are in line with current and anticipated team/organisational requirements

(b) Individuals are encouraged and assisted to evaluate their own learning and development needs and to contribute to the discussion, planning and review of development

(c) Plans contain clear, relevant and realistic development objectives and details of supporting development activities

(d) development activities optimise the use of available resources

(e) Plans are reviewed, updated and improved at regular intervals after discussion and agreement with the appropriate people

(f) Where development activities prove appropriate and/or the resources used are unsuitable or inadequate, realistic alternatives are discussed, agreed and implemented

Range Indicators:

This activity is carried out for individuals both:
- within the line responsibility of the manager
- determined by the organisation but for whom the manager does not have line responsibility, eg trainees.

Identification and review may take place during:
- induction
- periodic appraisals
- after promotion/relocation
- in response to particular requests or suggestions.

Development objectives and activities cover all areas in which individuals:
- need to develop to meet current and potential organisational objectives
- have career aspirations
- have a wider personal interest.

Development activities include:
- specifically allocated work activities
- formal education/training
- informal education/training

Approval, if required, for the use of resources is sought from:
- higher level managers
- colleagues, specialists, staff in other departments.

NVQ's are awarded by a variety of organisations approved by the National Council for vocational qualifications (NCVQ) or the Scottish Vocational Educational Council (SCOTVEC). The standards for a particular NVQ are defined by lead bodies of which there are currently around 160 in the U.K. The Management Charter Initiative (MCI) illustrated before is just one of these lead bodies.

Assessment for NVQ's does not consist of a one-off test or examination, instead it may involve a candidate in collecting evidence of competence to judge against the performance criteria, if necessary over a period of weeks or months. the emphasis on collecting evidence over a period of time means that the ability to demonstrate the competence can be applied in a variety of conditions and using a range of materials. Put another way, competence is inferred not from a single performance but from repeated performances.

Prior learning is also recognised under the NVQ system with accreditation possible for relevant past experience.

As well as the performance outputs, most NVQ's also incorporate an essential knowledge and understanding specification. This provides a purpose and context for the activity and ensures principles and methods are understood and background data is covered.

Personal competence may also be included, covering the ability of the individual to plan and analyse, manage others and manage themselves. The personal competences identified for managers are illustrated below:

Management Competences Project
Personal Competence Model

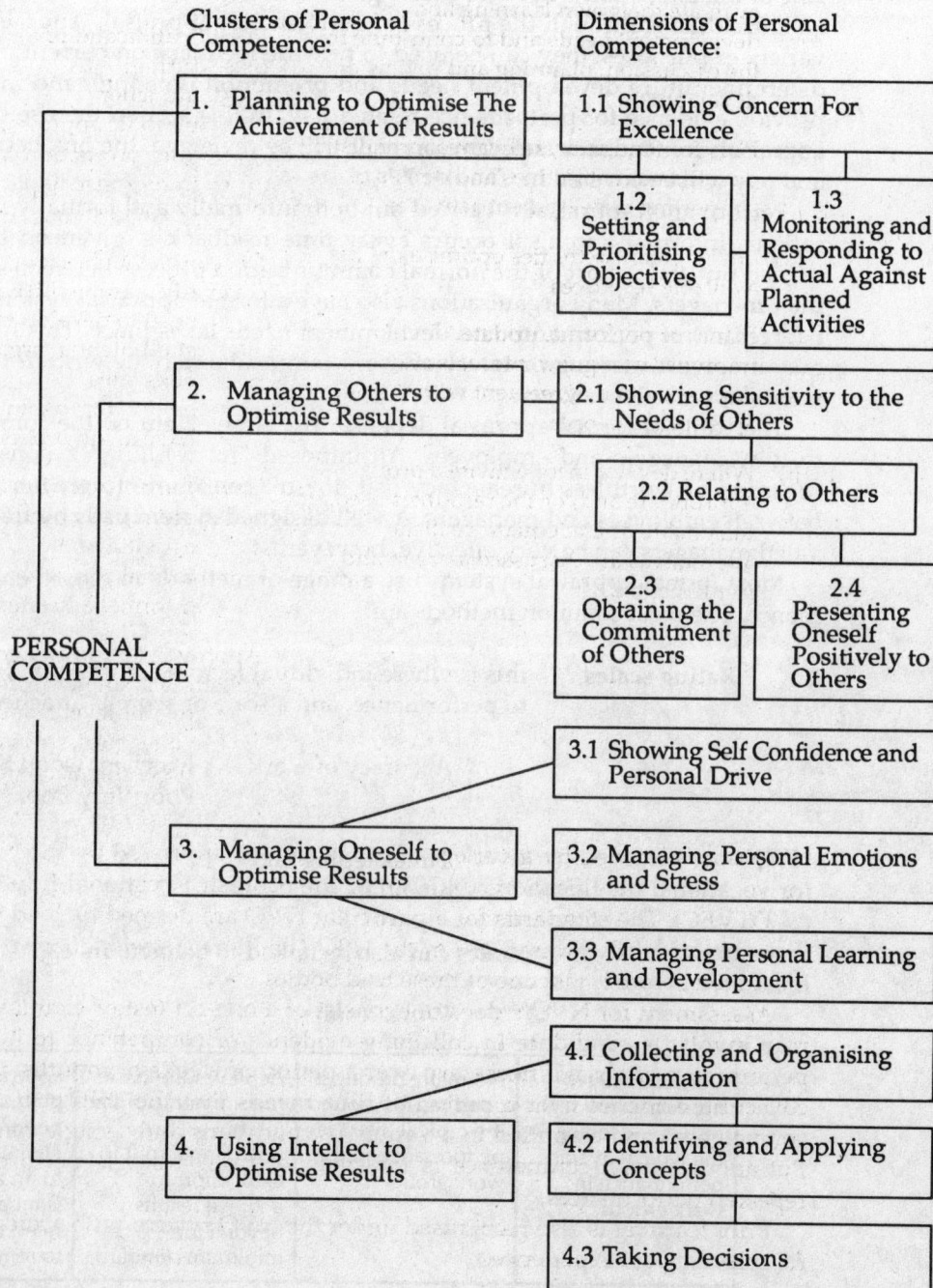

Clusters of Personal Competence:

Dimensions of Personal Competence:

PERSONAL COMPETENCE

1. Planning to Optimise The Achievement of Results

1.1 Showing Concern For Excellence

1.2 Setting and Prioritising Objectives

1.3 Monitoring and Responding to Actual Against Planned Activities

2. Managing Others to Optimise Results

2.1 Showing Sensitivity to the Needs of Others

2.2 Relating to Others

2.3 Obtaining the Commitment of Others

2.4 Presenting Oneself Positively to Others

3. Managing Oneself to Optimise Results

3.1 Showing Self Confidence and Personal Drive

3.2 Managing Personal Emotions and Stress

3.3 Managing Personal Learning and Development

4. Using Intellect to Optimise Results

4.1 Collecting and Organising Information

4.2 Identifying and Applying Concepts

4.3 Taking Decisions

In addition to the NVQ framework various other initiatives have also been introduced, particularly to assist those currently unemployed. Employment Training, Youth Training and the Job Club are some examples.

Nationally, vocational education and training are also supported by local Training and Enterprise Council's (TEC's). These are managed and run by business representatives to encourage and provide training and development within a particular regional area.

6.4 Performance appraisal

One of the important ways that training and development needs may be identified for an individual is through the process of performance appraisal. Appraisals can have a variety of purposes, they can be used to provide feedback on current performance, to determine future development needs and promotion potential, and in some cases to provide evidence for performance-related pay. In this section the use of performance appraisals for feedback and development will be reviewed, the link between appraisal and pay will be covered in Chapter 7.

Performance appraisal is carried out both informally and formally in most organisations. Informal appraisal occurs every time feedback is given on the work tasks carried out and is part of the normal communication process between employees and their managers. Many organisations also have a formal appraisal system where a periodic review of performance and development needs takes place. This formal appraisal may involve a meeting or interview, and the results may be written up on a performance appraisal form.

The value of formal appraisal depends to a large extent on the commitment given to it by managers and employees. An imposed "form-filling" exercise may well be regarded as worthless bureaucracy if it doesn't contribute to greater understanding between employees and managers. A well designed system used by trained and motivated managers can be very effective, however.

Most formal appraisal systems use a range of methods to record employee performance. The most common methods are:

1. **Rating scales**   this is where individual factors are identified that contribute to performance, and a scale or score is attached to them e.g.

Accuracy of work	Excellent Good Satisfactory Poor Very Poor
Timekeeping and attendance	1 2 3 4 5

Scales can also be linked to behaviours e.g.

Work results

Consequently produces very high results exceeding the typical average performance in work groups	Normally produces good results around the typical average performance in the work group	Achieves the basic requirements of the job but seems unwilling to put in extra effort to achieve results beyond the minimum standard	appears to have difficulty in performing some elements of the job to an acceptable standard and will need to take action to remedy problems

2. **Results orientated**   these are based on the setting of targets or objectives, which are also sometimes known as key results areas. For each employee targets or results areas are identified and agreed for a fixed period of time and performance is then assessed by the ability of the individual to meet or exceed the target. More detail on this process can be found in section 7.2

3. **Narrative or free written reports**   this is where the appraiser writes freely about the employee either in a totally unstructured way or sometimes semi-structured based on a number of headings.

4. **Comparative appraisal**   this is where the employee's performance is assessed relative to other members of his/her work group or department.

Activity

What are the advantages and disadvantages of each method?

Rating scales are fairly simple to fill out and provide standardised data. The criteria may be unclear or irrelevant, however, and the scoring method quite subjective. Most appraisers would need detailed training in order to be able to interpret the scoring system. Results orientated appraisals are effective and focus on the output of a job, but are less easy to use where the job tasks performed are difficult to quantify, and the individual's input or effort may be unrecognised. Where targets are set by mutual agreement this method may be highly effective. Narrative reports are less constrained and can focus on key performance issues, but there is a risk of subjectivity and inconsistency in the recording process. Comparative appraisals may be useful for determining promotion potential, but only tell you about relative performance. Most organisations opt for a combination of these methods in their appraisal forms.

As well as the methods of recording appraisal details most organisations conduct performance appraisal interviews to allow communication between the individuals. Some organisations have a closed system where the appraiser has already completed the assessment and simply communicates the outcome. More commonly, however, the appraisal interview is open and the interviewee is invited to share in the appraisal process.

An important preparation stage is to let the appraisee conduct a self-appraisal before the meeting so that thoughts and ideas he/she wishes to communicate can be organised. The appraisee should be encouraged to identify his/her own training and development needs. The appraisal interview should be conducted in a location without interruptions and the outcome should be clear to both parties. Basic data on job performance should be collected and any previous targets reviewed. Development needs for the future should be discussed and agreed and recorded on the appraisal form. Finally, new performance targets should be set for the next period.

When conducted in this way appraisal can be both motivating and informative.

6.5 Training needs and training plans

Training needs can be identified at various levels within the organisation. For an effective training needs analysis firstly organisational wide needs will have to be identified based on the corporate and HR plans. The needs of the whole organisation will then have to be translated into the needs of departments or work teams, and finally linked to the needs of individual employees.

Essentially, a training need occurs when the knowledge, skill or behaviour demanded exceeds current capabilities. The bigger the gap between the ideal and the actual level of performance the greater the training need.

Activity

List factors that could produce training needs that would affect the whole organisation?

For the organisation as a whole, training needs may arise from a whole variety of factors including:

- ❑ the introduction of new products/services
- ❑ re-organisation, mergers or sell-offs
- ❑ new legislation or changes in legislation
- ❑ the introduction of new technology
- ❑ quality initiatives
- ❑ customer service initiatives
- ❑ high labour turnover or low staff morale

Activity

How might team or department training needs be identified?

For a team or department the training needs would be identified by comparing the performance of the team against the targets or objectives set for it. Team needs may also be identified by the members of the team covering issues such as:

- ❑ team roles
- ❑ the organisation of work
- ❑ the quality of performance
- ❑ turnover levels and group morale

For an individual, training needs would arise from:

- ❑ the job requirements
- ❑ the outcome of performance appraisal

Training needs, at any level, need to be reviewed regularly to make sure they are updated.

Training needs then need to be formulated into training plans which outline the ways in which the needs will be met. Limited resources in most organisations mean that in many cases choices have to be made between the various needs and the priorities set. Training should not be seen solely as a remedial process, investment in training for high performing individuals may have a significantly greater pay off.

Activity

You are the manager of a small road haulage business. Of your 4 drivers 2 are rated good, 1 excellent and 1 less than satisfactory. You are able to fund one training course at the present time, and the choice is between:

1. a refresher HGV driving course
2. an advanced course which teaches the higher driving skills that ensure an excellent driver

Who would you select for training, and on which course? Give reasons.

This is obviously a difficult decision and the manager would need to assess clearly the relative needs both of the individuals and the organisation as a whole. Should the unsatisfactory driver be given the opportunity to take a refresher course to bring him/her up to an acceptable standard, or should a good driver be upgraded to excellent? The implications of not addressing the shortcoming of the unsatisfactory driver would need to be assessed. Is training a likely solution, or would disciplinary measures be more appropriate? These question indicate the need for a detailed level of analysis in order to make an informed choice.

6.6 Designing training and development programmes

Having established through analysis the training needs and training priorities of the organisation these plans now need to be translated into specific training and development programmes. When designing a training programme a series of questions need to be addressed:

1. Where will the training take place, at the workplace, off-the-job but within the organisation, or externally?

2. Who will be the trainer(s)?

3. Over what time period will the training/development take place?

4. What methods are appropriate?

5. What resources are needed?

The answers to these questions will help to establish the objectives and aims of the programme.

What would be the advantages and disadvantages of training at the workplace, training off-the-job but within the organisation, or externally?

Training at the workplace has the advantage of being real, immediate and practical. The trainee is able to practise what is learned straight away. Disadvantages could be that the training is fragmented and constantly interrupted, errors could cause real damage or customer annoyance, and the trainer may not be well qualified or motivated to provide high quality input. Off-the-job locations within the organisation allow some "time-out" for thought and analysis, and can provide a safe environment within which to practise new skills. There could be the benefit of a group of trainees working together, and a dedicated trainer. Disadvantages include the cost of the room and equipment together with the need to cover the trainees own jobs, and the possible difficulty of transferring the knowledge and skills acquired into the real work situation. External courses could be useful if specialist expertise or equipment is required, or if the organisation doesn't posses a training facility. External courses also allow the delegate to learn from those working in other organisations. Disadvantages include the cost of such programmes and in some cases the lack of relevance to the actual job performed.

Activity

Who could undertake the trainer role within the organisation?

Large organisations may have specialist full-time trainers and internal consultants to undertake training and development activities. Line managers and supervisors would also have a training role, and designated employees within the workforce may be used as trainers. At all these levels those involved with training should themselves receive help and guidance in how to train effectively. Communication skills and structured programmes would be needed. Informally, almost every individual will be called on to assist in the training of others at some point and the promotion of a helpful and supportive attitude will ensure a "learning culture" is achieved.

When considering the most appropriate training methods the time period over which the training/development will take place is very important. Some methods are more suited to short training courses, others are better for workplace training or longer term educational or development programmes. Some methods are more appropriate for gaining knowledge, others are better for skill development or behaviour modification.

Activity

Look at the list of training and development methods shown below, indicate for each whether you think they are:

i)   individual or group methods or could be used for both;

ii) used to impart knowledge, develop a skill, or facilitate behaviour change.

Job rotation	Case studies
Exercises	Handouts
Discussions	Coaching
Lectures	Video films
Demonstrations	Books/manuals
Seminars/workshops	Secondments
Simulations	Role plays
Team type/team role inventories	Projects

Individual methods	Group methods	Used for both
Job rotation Team type/team role inventories Handouts Books/manuals Secondments Projects	Lectures Seminars/workshops Discussions	Demonstrations Simulations Case studies Role plays Video films Exercises Coaching

Knowledge methods	Skill methods	Behaviour change methods	Used for knowledge, skill and behaviour change
Lectures Handouts Books/manuals	Demonstrations Simulations Role plays Coaching	Team type/team role inventories	Job rotation Seminars/workshops Case studies Video films Secondments Projects

For the acquisition of knowledge a combination of written and verbal material is normally most effective. Some learners prefer self-study materials which can be completed at the learners own pace, others prefer the support of groups. Skill training methods must allow the learner to practise in a safe and supported environment. Behaviour change methods help the learner identify and analyse current beliefs and behaviours and then modify them to gain maximum effectiveness.

From the choice of methods, the resource implications can be assessed and the programme costed.

6.7 Evaluation and feedback procedures

As outlined before, effective programme development must be linked to training needs defined in terms of objectives and aims. Where this has been done the evaluation process is fairly straightforward, the assessment is based around the extent to which the programme has met those needs.

If the objectives were quantifiable or measurable, at the end of the programme success could be evaluated by the ability of the individual to answer questions or perform a certain skill. Where the objectives were less measurable, however, the effects may be more difficult to perceive. For example, a course on assertiveness or team leadership may require a longer assessment period in order to evaluate its effectiveness.

Evaluation needs to take place at various time periods therefore, in order to see if there has been any lasting effect. Where individuals are supported in their learning by their line managers the effects of a programme may be much more noticeable. Most effective evaluation requires detailed monitoring and feedback over time.

Some organisations attempt to evaluate effectiveness in cost/benefit terms. There are substantial difficulties in detaching the effects of training from other variables, however.

Activity

You have just completed a course on keyboard skills for complete beginners. How could the effectiveness of the programme be evaluated?

One essential element would be to establish the initial skills of the learner, maybe by using a short exercise at the beginning of the course. As a short-term method of evaluation the same, or similar, test could be given at the end, and the progress noted. In the longer term the trainee should then be supported and evaluated back in their job so that the transferability of the programme could be assessed. A "control" could be set up with an operator who had not been on the training course to see if there were any differences in ability between them that could be attributed to the training. Feedback could also be invited on whether the course was long enough, whether the methods used were interesting, whether the trainer was effective etc?

As well as evaluation, the organisation will also need to assess the validity of the programme. To be valid the course must meet the needs outlined at the beginning. It is possible for a course to be effective and interesting, but not valid because the outcome was not what was intended.

6.8 Summary

In this chapter the essential elements of employee development have been covered. Theories about how people learn were introduced to show how motivation, structure and context influence the outcome of a training or development event. National educational and vocational programmes were described and the processes of performance appraisal and identifying training needs were covered. The construction of training plans and the design of training programmes were described, and finally the evaluation process was outlined.

Further reading

Cole G, *Personnel Management* (3rd edition) Chapters 23-31, DP 1993

Fletcher C, *Appraisal – Routes to improved performance*, IPD

Harrison R, *Training and Development*, IPD

Honey P, *Improve your people skills*, IPD

Mumford A, *Management Development* (2nd edition), IPD

Randell G, Packard P, and Slater J *Staff appraisal – A first step to effective leadership*, IPD

Reid M, Barrington H and Kenny J *Training interventions* (3rd edition), IPD

Wood S, *Continuous development*, IPD

Exercises

Progress questions

These questions have been designed to help you remember the key points in this chapter. The answers to the questions are on p126

Complete the following sentences:

1. Experiential learning can be analysed into 4 stages, these are......................................

2. NVQ's are divided into units which are then subdivided into.............., and ....

3. Comparative appraisal is a method which ....

4. A training need arises when ....

5. The most common methods used to convey knowledge are..

Select the correct responses to the following statements:

6. The NVQ qualifications can only be undertaken if you are in a job.

    True ☐ False ☐

7. Self appraisal is an important preparation stage before a performance appraisal interview.

    True ☐ False ☐

8. Coaching is an effective method of developing skills in a job.

    True ☐ False ☐

9. Validity is a measure of how well the participant enjoyed a course.

    True ☐ False ☐

10. The behaviourist approach to learning is based on the ideas of stimulus and response conditioning.

    True ☐ False ☐

Review questions

These questions have been designed to help you check your comprehension of the key points in this chapter. You may also wish to look further than the text in this chapter in order to answer *them fully. You will find your library useful as a source of wider reading. You can check the essential elements of your answerrs by referring to the appropriate section.*

11. What are the major theories covering how people learn? (Section 6.2)

12. Describe the structure and format of an NVQ (Section 6.3)

13. How can performance appraisals help identify training and development needs for an individual? (Section 6.4 and 6.5)

14. What are the main factors that need to be considered when designing a training/development programme? (Section 6.6 and 6.7)

Multiple choice questions

The answers to these questions are given in the Lecturer's Supplement.

15. Which of the following terms, used in the NVQ system, describes a discrete aspect of competence which can be certified independently:
    a) performance criteria
    b) unit
    c) range statement
    d) element

16. Cognitive theory:
    a) explains how memory operates
    b) is based on conditioning of behaviour
    c) describes how positive and negative feedback affects learning
    d) covers how ideas and theories are formulated

17. The term used to describe whether a course met its objectives is:
    a) reliability
    b) evaluation
    c) assessment
    d) validity

18. Which of the following training methods would be most suitable for conveying facts and knowledge?:
    a) role plays
    b) lectures
    c) group exercises
    d) demonstrations

Practice questions

A marking guide to these questions is given in the Lecturer's Supplement.

19. How would you identify the training needs for a team or a department?

20. Discuss how job rotation can help to develop knowledge, skills and behavior change.

21. How can training and development programmes be evaluated?

22. How do performance appraisals assist in the development of individuals?

Questions for advanced students

A marking guide to these questions is given in the Lecturer's Supplement.

23. How can theories of learning be linked to the design of training and development programmes?

24. Design an training programme to develop the ability to conduct performance appraisal interviews.

Assignment: Problems at Busy-buy supermarket

A marking guide to this assignment is given in the Lecturer's Supplement.

The Busy-buy supermarket store in Winchester has recently recruited a significant number of new check out operators because of an expansion in the size of the store. Of the 12 operators working on each shift half of them are new.

The new operators were trained for one day at the workplace by the existing staff.

At first all appeared to be going well, but last week there were several significant errors in the money held in the tills, and an increase in the number of customer complaints about their bills and the service they'd received.

Required

As the personnel/training officer responsible for the store you have been called in to investigate the problem.

i) outline how you intend to carry out the investigation, and suggest how any training needs could be identified;

ii) make recommendations on how the training of check out operators should be conducted in the future.

iii) detail how the training of the check out operators should be evaluated.

7 Performance and reward management

7.1 Introduction

This chapter looks at the way in which work performance is managed within an organisation. It begins by reviewing how work objectives are set for the organisation, team and individual and covers how work is planned, allocated and evaluated to meet these objectives. The feedback processes used to assist in performance management are then described together with a discussion on how work is valued for pay purposes. The chapter ends with a look at payment systems and other employee benefits.

This chapter provides coverage of the NVQ management unit "plan, allocate and evaluate work carried out by teams, individuals and self".

On completing this chapter you should be able to:

❑ set and update work objectives for teams, individuals and yourself;

❑ understand how to plan activities and determine work methods to achieve the objectives set;

❑ understand how to allocate work and evaluate teams, individuals and self against objectives;

❑ provide feedback to teams and individuals on their performance;

❑ understand the different ways in which work can be valued;

❑ describe and evaluate payment systems;

❑ describe and evaluate the use of employee benefits.

7.2 Managing work performance

One of the most important factors in determining an organisation's success is the way in which performance is managed. For performance management to be effective the following conditions must be met:

a) each individual must be aware of the results expected of him/her;

b) each individual's contribution must be linked and co-ordinated with that of others to achieve team and organisational results;

c) feedback, updating and monitoring must be undertaken regularly to review performance results.

To set work objectives for an individual the first requirement is to establish what the objectives of the group are and then break them down for each individual in the group. As we saw in Chapter 2.2 organisations may have a variety of structures and work groups, organised on different principles. Nevertheless, once the basic groupings have been established it should be possible to determine the key result areas by consulting the organisation's corporate plan. Key result areas are based on what the group has to achieve in output terms.

Examples of key result areas for a production department could include product quality, delivery accuracy, cost of production, employee safety etc. For a sales department they could be based on sales levels, customer base, sales costs etc. These result areas can then be translated into objectives or targets.

Good objectives are S.M.A.R.T. (an acronym for the following factors):

Specific	(clear and unambiguous)
Measurable	(the objective must contain a number, ratio or percentage, or it must be clear when it has been achieved)
Agreed	(by the individual, the manager and the team)
Reasonable	(objectives have to be achievable)
Time bound	(indicate "by when" an objective is to be achieved.)

Objectives should also be listed in order of priority to show the relative importance of each.

Some examples are shown below:

KEY RESULT AREA	MEASUREMENT METHOD	OBJECTIVE
Sales	Unit sales – Midland area	Unit sales of 1600 this year
Accidents	Accident rate	Decrease accidents by 5% in current year
Production costs	Variable cost/unit	To reduce to 80% of current costs by January next year.

Objectives should be set for the medium and longer term as well as the immediate short-term needs. They should also be reviewed, modified and updated regularly.

Activity

Which of the following would provide a good performance objective?

a) all orders must be achieved within 7 days;

b) customer satisfaction must be ensured at all times;

c) a pleasant and friendly telephone manner is required;

d) all letters to be responded to within one day of receipt.

a) and d) provide measurable, output based objectives, b) is not sufficiently quantifiable and c) relates to the input behaviour of the individual not to a performance output.

Having established performance objectives for the unit and for individuals, it is now necessary to determine the actual work methods to be used to achieve these objectives. This requires planning and considering the most effective work methods to use. Important factors include:

a) the degree of supervision needed by each individual in the team;

b) the equipment and materials required;

c) the training and development required;

d) the use of technology.

Further details on job design and work methods are covered in Chapter 3.4.

When allocating tasks to individuals the work allocation should optimise the use of resources and the existing competences of staff. Team and individual responsibilities and limits of authority should be clearly set, and the work allocated should ideally provide suitable learning opportunities for the employees concerned. It is most important that the work allocation is monitored to make sure the level and pace matches the capabilities of the individual. Where work allocations are not met, a full evaluation should result to establish the causes. Individuals must be encouraged to seek clarification if necessary about what is required of them.

Activity

You are the manager of a life-insurance department. Julia, a recently appointed clerical assistant, comes to see you in tears because of a back-log of work that she hasn't been able to process. She claims that she has been working unpaid overtime to try to catch up but is unable to cope with the job demands. Julia's supervisor says she is lazy and unco-operative and simply finds the work boring. How would you deal with the situation?

Obviously there could be a variety of factors that have contributed to this situation, but as the manager you would need to examine the work targets set for Julia and decide if they are realistic. Does she need additional training to help her improve her performance or should the targets be revised? The attitude of Julia's supervisor to performance management should also be examined. A counselling and supportive approach should be used in the first instance before assumptions are made that Julia is lazy.

This case study illustrates another vital part of performance management, the need to provide feedback to the individual on how he/she is doing. In section 6.4 performance appraisal systems were reviewed and different styles examined. Feedback on performance uses many of the same techniques as appraisal, but in this case the assessment is based solely on the evaluation of current performance. Where objectives or targets have been set performance is reviewed against them and feedback on the results given. The emphasis is on output results again rather than the input of the individual.

Effective feedback characteristics, from the MCI standards, include:

a) feedback should be given in sufficient detail, and in a manner and at a level and pace, appropriate to the individual(s);

b) feedback should be given at an appropriate time and place;

c) feedback should provide constructive suggestions and encouragement for improving future performance against work and development objectives;

d) feedback should recognise performance and achievement and encourage individuals to contribute to their own assessment;

e) feedback should ensure that details of any action to be taken is accurately recorded in line with organisational guidelines;

    f)   feedback should encourage and assist individuals to make suggestions on how systems/procedures could be improved.

7.3 Valuing work

As well as the performance management steps outlined in the previous section, the organisation will also need to devise an objective system with which to place a value on the job performed. This value can then be converted to a financial payment. This process is often referred to as job evaluation, although in reality value can be attached both to the job content and the personal contribution of the job holder. We saw in Chapter 5.2 the role of the Equal Pay Act (1970) in establishing the principle of equal pay regardless of sex, for work of equal value. The method by which a job is valued is, therefore, very important when determining equal pay cases. Even without this legal requirement most organisations would wish to base their payment systems on a fair and rational system, rewarding most those who contribute most. The four main methods of job evaluation are:

a) job ranking

b) job classification

c) points rating

d) factor comparison

The first two methods are non analytical, they are based on an overview of the whole job. The second two methods are analytical involving a more detailed breakdown of the job into its component parts. For Equal Pay cases, only the analytical methods are considered sufficiently well grounded to provide evidence of an objective approach. For any method of job evaluation the first essential requirement is an up to date job description on which to base the assessment, (see Chapter 3.4 for more detail on this process). Each job evaluation system is described briefly below:

1. *Ranking*

This method simply involves comparing one job description with another and arranging them in order of importance. Jobs may be compared with reference to a single factor like responsibility, or several factors such as decision-making, complexity, knowledge and skills, physical effort. To help the ranking process certain jobs may be chosen to provide "benchmarks" or indicators of various levels of importance. Jobs can then be slotted between these benchmark jobs until they have all been ordered. Once a rank order has been produced the jobs can then be divided up into grades or scales.

2. *Job classification*

This method defines the number of grades in the pay structure and then provides a description of the characteristics of the jobs found in each grade. Each job description is then compared to the grade descriptions and slotted in accordingly.

Activity

Into which grade would you place the job described below, using the basic classification system outlined?

Job: Clerical Assistant

Academic requirement 5 GCSE's at grade C. 2 year's general office experience. No supervisory responsibility. Some task variety under supervision.

Job classification system:

Grade 4   Professional/degree level qualifications. 5-10 year's experience, 2 or more in a specialist/managerial role. A department or team leader. Autonomous and multi-skilled.

Grade 3   2 A levels/GNVQ's. 5 year's experience some in a specialist/supervisory role. Minimal supervision needed and more complex tasks. Basic supervision of 1-2 others.

Grade 2   2-5 GCSE's at C grade. 6 months – 3 years generalist experience. Closely supervised with a range of tasks performed.

Grade 1   No formal academic qualifications or previous work experience. Fully supervised with basic tasks.

The job would be place in Grade 2 as the grade description closely matches that of the job to be valued.

3.   *Points rating*

Each job is broken down into a number of factors which are regarded as common to those jobs being analysed eg skills, responsibility, physical and mental requirements, working conditions. The number of factors is usually quite large. The factors are weighted to reflect the varying degrees of importance attached, and points are then awarded for each factor according to a pre-determined scale. Each job is then considered under each factor and points allocated. The total points gained by a job decides a job's place in the ranking order.

An example of how this works using just 2 factors is shown below:

Factor: COMPLEXITY OF DUTIES

Points:

0–15   Simple, repetitive or routine duties, requiring the use of definite procedures, and little individual judgement since the work is either done under immediate supervision or involves little choice as to method or performance.

16–30   Repetitive or routine duties, involving the use of various procedures and the application of clearly prescribed standard practice requiring the taking of minor decisions and the use of some judgment.

31–45   Diversified duties involving an intensive knowledge of a restricted field, requiring the use of a wide range of procedures, devising and recommending new methods or modifying standard processes and exercising judgment in the analysis of facts or circumstances surrounding individual problems to determine what action should be taken.

46–60 Wide variety of duties involving a definite knowledge and interpretation of company policies and procedures within scope of responsibilities and their application to cases not previously covered. Duties require considerable judgment to work independently toward general results, devising new approaches to problems, modifying or adapting standard procedures to meet new conditions, making decisions guided by precedent and based on company policies.

Factor: SUPERVISION RECEIVED

0–10 Under close supervision, with assignments of work at frequent intervals and a regular check of performance.

11–20 Under immediate supervision, where standard practice enables the employee to proceed alone on routine work, referring all questionable cases to supervisor.

21–30 Under direct supervision, where a definite objective is set requiring the use of a wide range of procedures and the employee plans and arranges his/her own work, referring only unusual cases to supervisor.

31–40 Under general supervision, working from policies or general objectives. Rarely refer specific cases to superior unless clarification or interpretation of company policies is involved.

41–50 Works under policy guidance only setting own standards within limit of budget or policy and is directly accountable for outcome.

The allocation of points for either of these factors would require the job description being compared with the point's score criteria to decide which band it falls in, and then deciding the actual points allocation by deciding whether it is nearer to the band below or the band above. The different points allocations between the two factors reflects the weighting the organisation gave to each. The results for two jobs could be:

JOB 1	Complexity of duties	40	
	Supervision received	35	Total = 75

JOB 2	Complexity of duties	14	
	Supervision received	20	Total = 34

Job 1 is therefore, valued more highly than job 2. Once the points ranking has been completed, grades and salary scales can be determined.

4. *Factor comparison*

Each job is analysed under a number of factors as in the point's rating method above. Key jobs (benchmark) jobs are then analysed and monetary values are attributed to the various factors eg

Job 1	Mental effort	£ 6,000
	Skill	£ 1,500
	Physical effort	£ 500
	Responsibility	£ 2,000
	Total salary	£ 10,000

Job 2	Mental effort	£12,000
	Skill	£ 4,000
	Physical effort	£ 500
	Responsibility	£10,000
	Total salary	**£26,500**

A monetary scale can then be built up for each factor, and other jobs analysed according to the factors and the benchmark jobs. The end result is a monetary ranking of jobs and a clear indication of how value relates to pay. The linking of monetary value to the job factors is a very complicated process, however, and would need to be updated frequently.

For all job evaluation methods the individuals who value the jobs should be selected so as to give as unbiased a view as possible of the relative merits of each job. A panel of 4-6 evaluators is often used drawn from management, trade unions and the workforce.

Job evaluation schemes can be fully customised for the organisation, or a consultancy can be used which provides a more standardised system. The choice of factors to be assessed and the scores awarded will always be a fairly subjective process. Unfair discrimination must be avoided and jobs reviewed regularly.

7.4 Payment systems

Converting the rank order of jobs determined from job evaluation into a sensible payment system is a complex and important process. A well designed payment system must:

a) be seen to reward employees for the skills and efforts they contribute;

b) provide a pay rate that is comparable to that paid by other organisations for similar work;

c) allow flexibility to reward performance individually.

Organisations must also be mindful of their overall ability to pay (profitability) and the requirements of the human resource plan in either attracting or reducing staff.

Traditionally there has been a separation in the methods of payment for blue-collar (production) workers and white-collar (managerial, professional and administration) workers.

Activity

Outline the traditional differences between the payment systems of manual workers and managers?

Traditionally, blue-collar workers would be paid by the hour, often in cash in a weekly pay packet. Pay is based on a flat rate (standard rate) for the job which does not vary according to the individual's skills or experience. Managers are more likely to be paid a monthly salary direct into a bank account, and progress through a career hierarchy based on age, seniority, qualifications, experience and performance factors.

Many organisations are recognising the limitations of this divided approach, and are beginning to harmonise payment systems (bring them both on to the same basis).

Harmonisation reduces the "them and us" conflicts of the past and leads to greater standardisation of systems.

A good payment system should provide for some progression in the job, often by means of incremental pay increases. These increases may be automatic made on an annual basis, or discretionary dependent upon assessed performance. The number of incremental steps in each pay grade needs careful determination and so does the process of moving from one pay grade to another. Some organisations have overlapping pay scales:

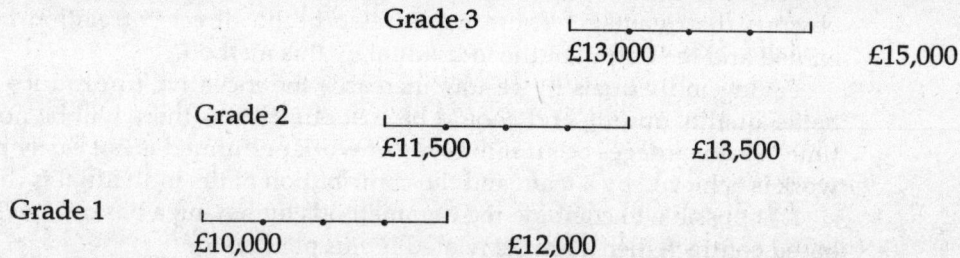

Grade 3
£13,000   £15,000

Grade 2
£11,500   £13,500

Grade 1
£10,000   £12,000

Movement from one grade to the next by this method requires a promotion to a higher graded (valued) job. The start point of the new salary can be adjusted to reflect experience and qualifications. By this method the pay of a very experienced Grade 1 job holder could be more than an inexperienced Grade 2 job holder. The top salary for each grade is set, and once the individual reaches this point no further pay increases will follow.

An alternative system uses continuous incremental points in a pay spine:

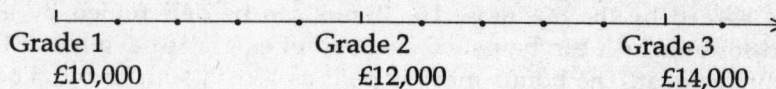

Grade 1   Grade 2   Grade 3
£10,000   £12,000   £14,000

An individual can progress up the pay spine without the need to be promoted to a different job. The organisation can then decide what is the maximum pay point for each job.

The basis of the payment system can be:

a) by time

b) by results

Time based systems base pay on the number of hours the employee attends the place of work. The contract of employment would normally set out the total number of hours to be worked and the method by which the hours will be distributed. As we saw in Chapter 2.2 time flexibility can be increased using methods such as flexi-time, annual hours, shift patterns and compressed working weeks. The mechanisms by which the hours worked are converted into the pay received may be quite complex particularly if overtime is used (enhanced pay for working more than a set number of hours per day or week). Employees may need to "clock in" to ensure the hours they work are recorded accurately, or their time-keeping must be closely supervised by management.

Results based systems depend not on the amount of time the employee spends at work, but on what they achieve whilst they are there. Pay is the result of the output achieved. Pay may be linked to both the quantity and quality of work produced.

Time based systems have the advantage of a more consistent and predictable pay rate for the employee and the guarantee that an employee will be at the workplace at fixed times. Where overtime is paid, however, employees may be motivated to take longer over their work in order to gain enhanced pay rates, which would be an obvious disadvantage. There would also be no direct correlation between the pay earned and the output of the individual by this method.

Paying individuals by results increases the incentive to produce more output or better quality output, and should be cost effective as there will be no pay for wasted time. Disadvantages occur if the type of work performed is not easily measured, or the work is achieved by a team and the contribution of the individual is difficult to assess.

It is possible to combine the two methods by having a basic wage linked to a time-based contract, then a results related bonus paid on top.

Results based systems can be designed for the following groups:

a) the whole organisation, through profit-related pay;

b) the work group, through team or department bonuses;

c) the individual, through piece-work, commission or performance-related pay.

All 3 methods can be used by the organisation if desired.

Profit sharing schemes pay a bonus to employees which is related in some way to the profits earned by the business. The bonus can be determined by a published and agreed formula or it can be issued as a sort of ex gratia payment at the discretion of the management. The bonus may be paid as a cash sum or by allocating shares to employees, or by a mixture of both.

Another advantage of using profit sharing schemes is to encourage involvement and interest in the operation and performance of the plant or company.

Group, section or department bonus schemes attempt to encourage flexibility and co-operation between members of the group. They can also, to some extent, provide opportunities for the employees to decide as a team how to achieve the required results. A disadvantage could be that competition or conflict is encouraged between different work groups which could be to the detriment of the organisation as a whole.

Individual bonus schemes can be based either on piece work (a payment for each unit produced) or by commission on sales. Targets may be set for standard performance (rewarded by basic pay) and then a bonus is paid for each additional item produced or sold. Alternatively, pay may be entirely based on output or sales.

Work measurement becomes of vital importance for either group or individual bonus schemes. The setting of the bonus levels and measurement of output can be a complex process.

The final form of individual payment system is performance-related pay which is a system of linking an individual's increases in salary to his/her assessed performance or merit rating. Section 7.2 demonstrated how performance assessment against objectives could be managed.

7.5 Employee benefits

As well as the payment system the organisation may use other forms of employee benefit (sometimes called fringe benefits). Reasons for using these include:

- to take advantage of tax concessions both for the employer and employee, particularly those on higher incomes;

- to provide benefits that assist the employee in their job, for example uniforms, health care and company cars for sales staff;

- to take advantage of economies the company can negotiate with suppliers as a bulk purchaser (car purchase, private health insurance etc)

- to utilise services and facilities already provided by the company e.g. insurance discounts, car purchase etc

- to enhance long term commitment to the organisation and reduce turnover by imposing a relatively large economic cost on leavers. This could be through mortgage subsidies or pension rights, or through the allocation of particular status benefits to longer serving employees (holiday entitlement, better company car etc).

Activity

List as many kinds of employee benefits as you can.

Some of the major employee benefits include:
- holiday entitlement
- pension schemes
- staff discounts on products and services
- housing assistance and mortgage subsidies
- private health care, dental treatment and eye tests
- hairdressing facilities
- subsidised meals and/or supply of restaurant facilities
- creches
- pleasant office facilities which may be used to denote a certain level of status
- company cars
- uniforms and other work equipment
- help with educational courses
- sabbaticals
- sports/social facilities

The benefits each individual would value depends to a large extent on their personal preferences and life stage. The desire for choice in employee benefits has been acknowledged by some companies who have set up "cafeteria benefit" schemes which operate by setting a price for each level of the selected benefits, expressed as credits, points or cash amounts. Employees can then decide which benefits they prefer and how to balance the amount of cash pay to benefits. The introduction of flexible benefit schemes:

❑ adds choice to the compensation package and aids retention and recruitment;

❑ offers employees the rewards they desire and so increases their motivation;

❑ maintains value for money with the benefits provided;

❑ helps create single status employment.

7.6 Summary

In this chapter the essential elements of performance and reward management have been covered. The process of setting work objectives, planning work methods and providing effective feedback for employees were covered. The chapter then looked at how work can be valued and described the job ranking, job classification, points rating and factor comparison methods. Payment systems were then reviewed and time-based and results-based methods described. Finally the use of employee benefits was discussed.

Further reading

Armstrong M & Murlis H (1991) *Reward Management: A Handbook of Remuneration Strategy and Practice*, (2nd edition) London, Kogan Page

Cannell M & Wood S, *Incentive Pay: Impact and Evolution*, IPD

Curson C, *Flexible Patterns of Work*, IPD

Thomason G, *Job Evaluation: Objectives and Methods*, IPD

Exercises

Progress questions

These questions have been designed to help you remember the key points in this chapter. The answers to the questions are on p126

Complete the following sentences:

1. The five characteristics of good objectives summed up in the acronym S.M.A.R.T. are...

2. Job classification is a method of job evaluation which..

3. The term harmonisation means...

4. A pay spine is...

5. Profit sharing payment schemes are...

Select the correct response to the following statements:

6. Job ranking is an acceptable way of valuing jobs for an equal pay claim.

    True ☐ False ☐

7. Factor comparison values work using monetary amounts.

    True ☐ False ☐

8. Shift payments are based on the results produced by the employee.

    True ☐ False ☐

9. Employee benefits may provide tax advantages for the employer and the employee.

    True ☐ False ☐

10. Holiday entitlement is an employee benefit.

    True ☐ False ☐

Review questions

These questions have been designed to help you check your comprehension of the key points in this chapter. You may also wish to look further than the text in this chapter in order to answer them fully. You will find your library useful as a source of wider reading. You can check the essential elements of your answers by referring to the appropriate section.

11. What are the characteristics of an effective performance feedback system? (Section 7.2)

12. What are the 4 main methods of job evaluation and how do they work? (Section 7.3)

13. Describe the main methods of paying for results that can be used by an organisation. (Section 7.4)

14. List the potential advantages of using a "cafeteria benefits" system. (Section 7.5)

Multiple choice questions

The answers to these questions are given in the Lecturer's Supplement.

15. Points rating:
    a) is a non-analytical job evaluation method
    b) involves comparing jobs with grade/class descriptions
    c) allocates a monetary value to each job factor
    d) uses number scores to show the value of each factor in the job

16. A benchmark job is:
    a) one used for job analysis
    b) used to mark a particular level of value in a job evaluation scheme
    c) used to harmonise payment systems
    d) a manual, blue-collar job

17. Which of the following is a time-based payment system:
    a) individual incentive bonus payment
    b) shift allowance
    c) profit-sharing
    d) performance-related pay

18. Performance objectives are:
    a) a measure of the individual's effort and skill
    b) a way of valuing work
    c) output measures against which performance can be compared
    d) used to determine employee benefits

Practice questions

A marking guide to these questions is given in the Lecturer's Supplement.

19. Outline how to set effective performance objectives for individuals and teams.

20. Discuss the advantages and disadvantages of points rating as a job evaluation method.

21. What are the characteristics of a harmonised payment system?

22. Evaluate the use of employee benefits within an organisation.

Questions for advanced students

A marking guide to these questions is given in the Lecturer's Supplement.

23. Set yourself some key results areas or performance objectives to achieve over the next 6 months. Are they S.M.A.R.T.?

24. Outline the forms of payment system you think would be the most suitable for the following groups of workers, with reasons:
    i) a manager of a life insurance department
    ii) a car assembly-line worker
    iii) a teacher/lecturer
    iv) a shoe shop assistant

Assignment: *Evaluating pay at Johnson's Machine Tools Ltd*

A marking guide to this assignment is given in the Lecturer's Supplement.

You are the Managing Director of Johnson's Machine Tools Ltd a medium size manufacturing company based in Manchester. You employ 250 staff, 60 are office workers and managers, 20 are technical/professional staff and the remaining 170 are assembly line skilled, semi-skilled and manual workers. The assembly line staff are paid weekly with pay based on an hourly rate monitored by a clocking system. The workers also have a group bonus system based on total output each week. Overtime and shift allowances are paid. There are few employee benefits for this group, a pension scheme does exist for all staff, however.

The other clerical, management, technical and professional staff are salaried, paid monthly and do not qualify for overtime. There are no incentive bonus schemes but a wide range of employee benefits are open to them, including company cars, private health insurance, and extra holiday entitlement, depending on status and position.

Currently job evaluation is done on a simple job classification basis with jobs slotted into the 3 worker grades, and 4 managerial/professional/clerical grades.

Required

As Human Resource Director you have been asked to evaluate the current systems and make recommendations to the Board of Directors in the following areas:

i) Does the organisation currently ensure equal pay for work of equal value?

ii) What are the advantages and disadvantages of harmonising the payment and benefit system for all employees?

iii) How could pay be better linked to performance in the organisation?

8 *Employee relations*

8.1 Introduction

This chapter looks at the ways in which relationships between the employer and employee are conducted, both individually and collectively. The chapter begins by tracing the history and importance of trade unions and looks at industrial relations issues today. The processes of negotiation and collective bargaining are reviewed, together with those involved with communication, consultation and participation more generally. The important role of U.K. law in the area of labour relations is reviewed, the rights of trade unions, companies and individuals are outlined. Particular issues of grievance, discipline and dismissal are covered in detail, and the management of health and safety at work reviewed.

This chapter provides coverage of the NVQ management unit "create, maintain and enhance effective working relationships."

On completing this chapter you should be able to:

❏ understand the role, power and importance of trade unions in the 1990's;

❏ prepare a case in order to conduct a negotiation and understand the processes involved in reaching agreement;

❏ outline various communication methods, and understand the benefits of employee consultation and participation;

❏ detail the main provisions of U.K. law in respect to trade union and individual rights;

❏ analyse a disciplinary or grievance incident and proceed in accordance with the ACAS guidelines and employment law;

❏ understand what is required to ensure health and safety at work.

8.2 Trade unions

The definition of a trade union given in the Trade Union and Labour Relations (Consolidation) Act 1992 states that a trade union is "an organisation (whether permanent or temporary) consisting wholly or mainly of workers of one or more descriptions whose principal purpose includes the regulation of relations between workers of that description and employers or employers' associations."

Trade unions can be regarded therefore, as any group of workers who combine together, even for brief periods, to secure something from an employer. The more usual impression of a trade union, however, is of a large, permanent organisation which is independent of the employer and involved with maintaining and improving the terms and conditions of its members. Trade unions need to register with the Certification Officer to gain recognised legal status. A union will be issued with a certificate of independence if it can demonstrate that its activities are not determined by an employer or employers.

The number and size of trade unions has changed significantly in the last 100 years. At the beginning of the century there were over 1200 different trade unions, mostly based on particular trades or crafts. Gradually, general unions emerged that recruited unskilled workers (one of these the Transport and General Workers Union

TGWU was the largest trade union until 1993). Trade unions were also based on recruitment from particular industries eg the mineworkers (National Union of Mineworkers NUM) or the railways (National Union of Railwaymen NUR).

Over the century from 1920 onwards the total number of trade unions has fallen dramatically. By the 1970's there were about 500 unions which has now reduced to 267 in 1994. The reason for this has been the increasing pace of mergers and amalgamations which form fewer but larger trade unions overall. In 1994 80% of all trade union members were concentrated into the top 19 trade unions. The merger in 1993 of the National Association of Local Government Officers (NALGO), the National Union of Public Employees (NUPE) and the Confederation of Health Service Employees (COHSE) formed the single largest trade union UNISON with a total membership of 1,464,931.

The number of workers who belong to trade unions has also altered over time. Up until the end of the 1970's total membership (with a few fluctuations between the wars) increased to a peak of 13 million in 1980. From the 1980's onwards total membership has fallen to the current figure of 8,665,944 at the end of 1994.

Activity

Outline the reasons why you believe trade union membership has fallen in recent years.

This is a complex issue but the main factors are:

1. the general economic recession of the late 1980's and 1990's with resulting redundancies and stronger management controls;

2. the re-structuring of the U.K. economy from the manufacturing sector (with higher unionisation rates) to the service and information technology sectors (with much lower trade union membership);

3. the breakdown of large, centralised corporations into smaller trading units. Trade union membership tends to be higher in larger organisations;

4. the demographic changes which include a greater proportion of female and part-time workers (often less trade union orientated), the early retirement of older workers (trade union members included) and the relatively low rate of trade union membership in the young (under 25 years);

5. the effects of government policy since 1979 which strongly discourages trade union intervention, together with the increasing restraints placed on trade unions by new employment laws.

It should be noted, however, that declining trade union membership is an international trend not one which affects the U.K. alone. The HRM perspective outlined in Chapter 1 also focuses much more on individual rather than collective mechanisms.

Trade unions operate in a variety of ways, but most have elected shop stewards at plant level, who report to full-time trade union officials regionally and then nationally. The shop steward will be the first point of contact for most employees, and has a valuable role in liaising with management. Unions have a rule book which sets out the framework within which their members and officials must operate.

Activity

Write to one of the top 10 trade unions and ask for their recruitment literature and rule book. This will give you a broader idea of the role and function of a trade union.

Most larger trade unions are also affiliated to the Trade Unions Congress (TUC). The TUC is an organisation which all unions can join. It's principal aim is to formulate collective policy which can then be used as the voice of the trade union movement as a whole. The TUC has an important role as spokesbody for the movement particularly in relation to government policy. The TUC is not directly linked to the Labour party, individual unions may set up political funds to support any political party if they wish. The TUC's role in trade union affairs is advisory only, it has no legal powers, the most major sanction that can be imposed is to expel a member union from the TUC if the rules have been broken.

8.3 Negotiation and collective bargaining

In order for a union to engage in negotiation with an employer it first has to be recognised. The recognition of a trade union by an employer is not a legal right it is a voluntary arrangement which the employer may, or may not, be prepared to enter into. A request for recognition would be more likely to succeed if the union could demonstrate that a significant number of employees were union members. On occasions there have been recognition disputes between trade unions over the right of representation. The TUC has a code of practice based on the Bridlington agreement which does not allow a union to recruit members when another union already has recognition rights. Some organisations have also de-recognised unions as part of a management change programme.

Where a trade union or trade unions are recognised collective bargaining may take place.

Activity

Explain what the term collective bargaining means to you.

Collective bargaining occurs when an employer (or group of employers) negotiates the terms and conditions of employment of their workforce with the representatives of one (or several) worker's organisations and reaches agreement on these issues. This means that various aspects of a worker's contract of employment are determined not individually, but collectively. The outcomes of collective bargaining are:

❑ substantive agreements – based on pay and terms and conditions of employment;

❑ procedural agreements – which set out an agreed course of action for various eventualities such as equal opportunities, recruitment, redundancy, discipline etc.

The terms of collective agreements will often affect all employees, not just those who belong to the trade union. As a result collective bargaining can have an impact far greater than that suggested by the level of trade union membership.

For collective bargaining to take place bargaining units need to be established. These units can be small work groups at a local level right through to national units representing hundreds of thousands of workers. The relationship between local bargaining and national bargaining has varied over time.

Activity

What are the main advantages of centralised national bargaining and how can these be compared with the advantages of de-centralised local bargaining?

Where collective bargaining takes place nationally terms and conditions of employment can be fixed for a whole sector of the labour market, reducing the effects of local wage competition. The power of such a bargaining unit is considerable and basic national rates provide stability and a guaranteed minimum wage for the membership. Local bargaining units, however, allow a more varied range of outcomes and greater local flexibility. They may also be more responsive to local needs. Currently the tendency has been towards more decentralised bargaining units.

Individual organisations may bargain separately with each recognised trade union, or arrange single-table bargaining where the representatives of all the trade unions sit down together with management. The advantage of single table bargaining is that the negotiations are integrated, but it may be more difficult to come to an agreement that satisfies all parties.

The process of collective bargaining is conducted by negotiation which can be defined as the discussion of matters with a view to reaching agreement. Negotiation can take place in 2 main ways:

1. through distributive bargaining where negotiation is based on the distribution of limited resources (one party's gain is another's loss, or WIN:LOSE bargaining);

2. through integrative bargaining, based on joint problem-solving, where negotiations aim to find a mutually satisfying solution to problems (WIN:WIN bargaining).

Formal negotiations often follow the same broad stages:

Preparation:

❏ set objectives. These are normally prioritised into three levels, the basic minimum requirements that must be achieved, the desirable requirements that the negotiator would like to achieve, and the optimum requirement or best level of achievement;

❏ research the background to the negotiation including the bargaining power of the other party. Prepare the case to be argued;

❏ select the negotiators who should be good communicators, persuasive, acceptable to the other party, and authoritative.

Negotiation

❏ exchange information;
❏ listen to the other party's position;

❑ signal likely compromise points;

❑ propose ways forward.

Closing

❑ summarise positions;

❑ propose a final offer which meets the needs of both parties;

❑ reach agreement.

Activity

Think of the last time you sold an item:

What was your initial position (ideal, good, and minimum requirement)?

How did the negotiation proceed?

What was the eventual outcome?

By analysing your negotiations you can identify where success or failure occurs.

Within the negotiation and collective bargaining framework there is potential for conflict. Bargaining allows these conflicts to be voiced and regulated and so provides a constructive organisational system. There may be occasions where conflict is not resolved through negotiation so both parties may use further sanctions to increase the power of their position.

Activity

What sanctions could be used by the trade union and the employer in furtherance of a dispute?

Trade union sanctions include:

❑ strikes

❑ overtime bans

❑ work-to-rule

❑ go slows

❑ sit ins

❑ boycotts

❑ ballots

❑ picketing

Employer sanctions include:

❑ lockouts

❑ lay-offs

❑ dismissal

The legality of some of the trade union and employer sanctions will be examined further in section 8.5, the purpose of using sanctions will be to cause maximum inconvenience to either party to persuade them to return to negotiations, and/or concede some further points. Sanctions may be damaging and costly to both parties and are normally only used in extreme circumstances.

The techniques used to resolve such disputes include:

☐ conciliation; where an independent third party acts as a go-between in order to help achieve a settlement between the two parties;

☐ mediation; where a third party has a more active role in proposing recommendations for both sides to consider;

☐ arbitration; where a third party settles the dispute by making an independent decision for the parties in dispute.

ACAS (the Arbitration, Conciliation and Advisory Service) provide specialist help in such circumstances.

8.4 Communication, consultation and participation

As we saw in the previous section, negotiation and collective bargaining provide one way of resolving conflict and forming agreements within organisations. Other methods can also be used to ensure clear two-way workplace communications which provide a channel for more individualised relationships between employer and employee. The move away from collective bargaining towards a more personal HRM approach particularly advocates the use of direct workplace communication. Communication involves the sharing of ideas, plans and targets throughout the workforce and involves both a vertical dimension (up and down the organisational hierarchy) and a horizontal dimension (between peers). Communication may be both verbal, through briefings, meeting and discussions, and written using bulletins, reports, memos, letters and company documents such as the contract of employment and staff handbook.

The degree to which employees are consulted on management decisions reflects the culture of the organisation. Consultation allows all points of view to be heard and taken into consideration before a decision is made. As a result the employees may feel more committed to the decisions made, and fear change processes less. Employee participation allow the employees to actually participate in management decisions, not just to be consulted on them. The degree of participation and the processes to support it vary. Full participation could involve employee representatives on company boards as in Germany (industrial democracy) but more usually involves employee participation on committees or project teams.

The right of employees to information and to have a say in how their organisation is run, is promoted in E.U. law. The U.K. is resisting these participation proposals preferring a less legalistic approach. The degree to which trade unions have been replaced by other mechanisms in recent years, shows the changes that are currently taking place in British industrial relations.

8.5 Labour law

Throughout the textbook references have been made to the role of employment law in regulating relationships between employers and employees. Labour law can be divided into two main areas:

1. individual labour law;
2. collective labour law.

Activity

Which areas of individual labour law have already been covered in the text?

The areas of individual labour law that have already been covered are:

❏ the contract of employment (4.4)

❏ equal opportunities (5.2)

❏ data protection (3.5)

❏ access to medical records (4.3)

The other main areas where the rights of the individual are covered in law are:

Dismissal/redundancy – see section 8.6

Union membership rights – The Trade Union and Labour Relations (Consolidation) Act 1992 provides the right for individuals to belong or not to belong to a trade union as they choose. It is illegal to dismiss or discriminate against an employee either because they are a trade union member or because they refuse to join a trade union. The Employment Act 1990 also increased the protection to include recruitment and selection. It is currently illegal to refuse employment to somebody because they are a trade union member, or because they refuse to join a trade union. This means that closed shop arrangements, where the employees are all required to join the union, are no longer lawful. The Trade Union Reform and Employment Rights Act 1993 also gives individuals the right not to be excluded or expelled from a trade union except for certain permitted reasons.

Time off work – The Trade Union and Labour Relations (Consolidation) Act 1992 created the legal right for an employee to take reasonable time off for trade union and public duty activities.

Maternity benefits – The Trade Union Reform and Employment Rights Act 1993 established the right for all pregnant employees, regardless of their length of service or hours of work to have 14 week's statutory maternity leave during which all their non-wage contractual benefits must be maintained. This is in addition to the right under the Trade Union and Labour Relations (Consolidation) Act 1992 to:

❏ a longer period of maternity absence of up to 29 weeks after the birth for qualifying employees (those who have two years continuous employment and work to the eleventh week before the expected date of confinement);

❏ paid time off work for ante-natal care;

❏ not be dismissed because of pregnancy (subject to the normal 2 year qualification period for the right not to be unfairly dismissed);

❏ receive 18 week's statutory maternity pay for qualifying employees (those who have 26 weeks continuous service, earn not less than the lower earnings limit for national insurance purposes, and work up until the eleventh week before the expected date of confinement).

Statutory sick pay – Employees have the right to statutory sick pay after the first 3 days of absence from work paid via the employer for 28 weeks (and the D.S.S. thereafter). This statutory sick pay is recoverable by the employer by offsetting payments against national insurance.

Medical suspension/guarantee payments – Where the employee is unable to work because the employer puts them on short-time work or lays them off, or where they are suspended on medical grounds, there is the right to receive payments providing the employee meets the basic qualifying requirements (ie has worked for 4 weeks or more in continuous service for 16 hours or more per week, or has 5 years continuous service and works 8 hours or more per week). For guarantee payments there are exclusions if the contract was to perform a specific task and was based on a fixed term of 3 months or less, or those whose contract of employment does not specify regular hours of work. Employees are not entitled to payments if they unreasonably refuse an offer of alternative employment. Medical suspension payments can only be made for the industries and occupations specified in the health orders in Schedule 1 of the 1978 Employment Protection (Consolidation) Act, and by those codes of practice issued under Schedule 16 of the Health and Safety at Work Act 1974.

Collective labour law:

Trade union immunities – When an individual goes on strike he/she has broken the contract of employment and could be sued by his/her employer. This situation would result in employees having very little power in collective bargaining so the idea of immunity from prosecution was introduced for certain acts. Under the Trade Union and Labour Relations (Consolidation) Act 1992 an act carried out in contemplation or furtherance of a trade dispute between employees and their employer would be covered by individual immunity. Secondary action, which is action against another employer, not your own, would not be protected from prosecution. The definition of a trade dispute is " a dispute between workers and their employer and related wholly or mainly to:

❑ the terms and conditions of employment or the physical conditions of work;

❑ engagement, non-engagement, termination or suspension of employees;

❑ allocation of work between employees or groups of employees;

❑ discipline;

❑ membership or non-membership of a trade union;

❑ facilities for trade union officials;

❑ the machinery for negotiation or consultation including trade union recognition.

Disputes between trade unions, or between one group of workers and another are not covered by immunity from prosecution.

Trade unions as a collective body have the same rights of immunity as an individual. The union has an extra requirement, however, to hold a secret ballot of all its members before any industrial action takes place. There are precise arrangements for this ballot and if these are not complied with the union will lose its immunity. Before an action takes place the union must authorise it, un-official action occasionally occurs where a shop steward or group of trade union members decide to strike without gaining the authorisation of the trade union. Under the Trade Union and Labour Relations (Consolidation) Act 1992 the union is liable for such un-official actions unless it issues a formal repudiation to the individuals concerned. Notice of the ballot, stating the date of the ballot and the employees who will be entitled to vote must be sent to the employer not later than 7 days before the ballot takes place. Not later than 3 days before the ballot a sample voting paper must be sent to the employer. For a ballot of more than 50 members an independent scrutineer must be appointed from those specified in an order made by the Secretary of State. The ballot must include all those members who will be called upon to take part in the industrial action. Voting must be by the marking of a voting paper containing questions framed so as to require a yes or no answer. The voting paper must contain the phrase "If you take part in a strike or other industrial action, you may be in breach of your contract of employment." Legally this means that striking employees can be dismissed for breach of contract. If the employer takes this step all the employees involved in the dispute must be dismissed, and if there is a subsequent re-instatement of the employees again all must be re-employed.

Majority support must be obtained in the ballot in response to the questions set for the industrial action to go ahead. Complaints by union members about trade union ballots or industrial action can be addressed to the Commissioner for the Rights of Trade Union Members, a government funded body. Employers may seek a court injunction if they believe the trade union has not conducted a secret ballot or dispute correctly. If the union breaches a court injunction they may be fined, and if the union refuses to pay a sequestration order may be awarded which compulsorily seizes union funds. This happened in the National Union of Mineworkers dispute with the Coal Board in 1984, with very damaging consequences.

Picketing – As a form of sanction, picketing is designed to provide a way to communicate with workers and ask them to abstain from work. The Employment Act 1980 restricted picketing to the employee's own place of work and the Code of Practice on picketing makes the following recommendations:

- the number of pickets at an entrance to a workplace should be limited to what is reasonably needed (as a general rule no more than 6 individuals);

- an experienced person, preferably a trade union official should always be in charge of the picket line;

- the organiser should ensure that the picket is peaceful and lawful, distribute identification for authorised pickets, and refuse outside support;

- a trade union member who crosses an unofficial picket line should not be disciplined by the union;

- pickets should ensure that the movement of essential goods and services is not impeded or prevented.

Activity

Which of the following examples is a lawful activity and which is not?

a) Ambulance workers coming out on strike in support of a nurse's pay dispute.

b) Members of the MSF union staging a 1 day sit-in without a union ballot.

c) Striking lorry drivers from a Manchester haulage company picketing a rival firm who had taken on their deliveries.

d) An employer dismissing all the workers on strike for breach of contract.

Both a), b) and c) are unlawful activities. In a) the ambulance workers would not normally be part of the same work group as the nurses, so as the dispute does not affect their own terms and conditions of employment they would be taking secondary action if they went on strike which is not covered by immunity. In b) the sit-in must be authorised by a properly conducted secret ballot to be lawful. In c) picketing may only be carried out at the individual's own place of work.

d) is a lawful situation, an employer may dismiss workers for striking providing all the workers are dismissed.

Industrial Tribunals

Most labour law cases are heard by an Industrial Tribunal. A tribunal has the functions of a civil court to enforce the law but is not restricted by the rules and procedures of an ordinary court. A tribunal is composed of:

- ❏ a legally qualified chairperson who directs activities;
- ❏ an employer representative; chosen from a Confederation of British Industry (C.B.I.) list;
- ❏ a union representative; chosen from a T.U.C. list.

The hearings are in public, parties can represent themselves or have others, including lawyers appear for them. The tribunal will make a judgment and award a compensatory financial sum where appropriate. Industrial tribunal decisions are not enforceable as ordinary court orders (through contempt laws), but if an employer refuses to comply additional financial penalties may be imposed. Appeals against an Industrial Tribunal ruling can only be made on a point of law. These are made to the Employment Appeal Tribunal in the first instance then ultimately to the Court of Appeal and the House of Lords.

8.6 Grievance, discipline and dismissal

In regulating the relationship between employer and employee there is a need for mechanisms that will help if the relationship breaks down. The basis for the relationship in law, is the contract of employment and the company's rules covering conduct and behaviour in employment. In most cases the normal communication channels should ensure that any difficulties are resolved informally between the individual and his/her line manager. Where this does not occur more formal procedures may be used. For the employee the main source of further action would be through the grievance procedure, for the employer through the disciplinary procedure.

Grievance procedure – This is a system which provides a method for employees to raise issues with management before they escalate into major disputes or result in the employee resigning. As such, management must ensure that grievances are heard speedily and impartially, and that action is taken as a result. In most procedures the first stage is to raise the issue formally with the line manager and for an interview to take place which defines the problem and moves towards an acceptable solution. Grievances may be raised about pay or other terms and conditions of employment, or behaviour such as harassment or race/sex discrimination. The interviewer needs good communication and counselling skills to identify the problem and determine what future action is needed. Grievance procedures should allow the right of appeal to a higher level of management if the individual feels that their grievance has not been dealt with adequately.

Disciplinary procedure – Where an improvement is required the employee must be made to clearly understand what needs to be done, how performance and conduct will be reviewed, and over what time period. Criticisms should be constructive and a two way discussion should take place to encourage improvement and find ways in which the employee can remedy any shortcomings. As with the grievance procedure many issues can be resolved by the use of counselling and communication between individuals and their employers.

Before disciplinary procedures can be formulated the organisation needs to establish a set of rules on conduct and performance.

Activity

What rules do you feel should be written down and communicated to all employees?

Obviously it is impossible to write rules to cover every situation but the ACAS Advisory Handbook on Discipline at Work recommends that rules should cover the following areas:

❑ timekeeping;

❑ absence;

❑ health and safety;

❑ gross misconduct (the kind of offences resulting in instant dismissal should be noted);

❑ use of company facilities;

❑ discrimination.

Activity

An ACAS model disciplinary procedure was used as an example in chapter 1.3. Familiarise yourself with the procedure and then suggest what you might do in the following circumstances:

a) Mary Jones, a previously reliable worker, arrives late for the fifth time in two weeks;

b) Joe Smith and Harry Longdon are found fighting in the loading bay;

c) Jennifer Redwood has been smoking in a prohibited area;

d) John Kelley is rude and abusive to a customer.

There is rarely one best way of handling these incidents; a lot will depend on the organisation's own custom and practice and the manager's personal style. In a) the counselling approach may well be the most suitable to establish if there are any particular circumstances affecting Mary Jones currently. If absence or lateness becomes a problem it should be closely monitored and the employee taken through the stages of the disciplinary procedure. In b) the seriousness of the offence could justify disciplinary action. If it was a minor incident an informal or verbal warning could be issued, if more serious or if health and safety were put at risk a formal warning and/or suspension of the individual would be appropriate. In c) if Jennifer Redwood has caused a major health and safety risk summary dismissal for gross misconduct could result. The organisation would need to show that this penalty would be applied to all employees in a consistent way for the dismissal to be fair. Alternatively, a formal written warning could be given with a tightening up of awareness of all health and safety rules implemented. In d) John Kelley would probably receive a formal written warning as rudeness to a customer is a serious offence. He may also benefit from counselling and training to help him react more constructively to stressful situations.

Dismissal – The ultimate penalty of a breach of discipline is dismissal. The rights of the employee are covered clearly in the Employment Protection (Consolidation) Act 1978 which states that to be fair dismissal must:

1. be for a valid reason;
2. the employer must have acted reasonably.

The fair reasons for dismissal laid down by law are:

❐ capability or qualification

❐ conduct

❐ redundancy

❐ statutory reason

❐ some other substantial reason

Activity

What do you think is covered by each of the above reasons?

Capability is the ability of the individual to do the job. If the work produced is of a poor quality or the individual is inefficient, they can be fairly dismissed. A tribunal would expect the individual to have been recruited and selected sensibly and given sufficient training to perform the job. Once a problem has been identified the individual should be given a chance to improve and further help given, unless the damage that is being caused is unreasonable and the employee cannot be allowed to continue. Capability also covers situations where an employee can no longer perform their job because of illness or disability. In these situations if it is possible to move the employee to more suitable work this should be done. Many companies will have sickness schemes which allow the individual considerable time away from their job. In smaller companies or in key jobs it would, however, be fair to dismiss an employee who was too ill or disabled to perform their job. If an individual claims that he/she has a qualification which turns out later to be untrue this is also a fair reason for dismissal.

Conduct reasons for dismissal include lateness and absence, fighting, drunkenness, indiscipline, lack of care, theft, fraud and breaking company rules. The disciplinary procedure of the organisation should be followed in these instances except in cases of gross misconduct when dismissal without notice may be an appropriate sanction.

Redundancy is a particular form of dismissal where the job an employee performs is no longer required by the organisation. The Employment Protection (Consolidation) Act 1978 provides the following rights for redundant workers:

❐ time off for job search or to attend an interview;

❐ a minimum redundancy payment based on length of service and salary at the time of redundancy (this is often enhanced by the employer).

Redundancy may be compulsory or voluntary. In voluntary redundancy situations individuals are invited to apply for redundancy.

Statutory reasons cover any situation where performing the job would involve breaking the law, for example if a lorry driver was banned from driving for drunkenness.

Some other substantial reason (S.O.S.R.) is a category used where the tribunal thinks the reason was fair but it does not fit into one of the categories above. The employer must demonstrate that the reason for dismissal is substantial and not trivial or frivolous. Some examples of fair reasons for dismissal brought under S.O.S.R. include:

❑ where a negotiated change in the terms and conditions of employment had been accepted by the majority of employees but not by one individual who refused to agree to the change. The employee was dismissed and this was found to be fair;

❑ where an employee with access to confidential data was closely associated with another individual who worked for a rival business and the employer had grounds for believing a substantial risk to the business existed;

❑ where a third party, who was a valued customer, put substantial pressure on the employer to dismiss an employee they disliked.

In establishing whether dismissal was fair the tribunal will also want to ensure that the employer acted reasonably. The employer is expected to follow the disciplinary procedure and rules of the organisation and issue warnings and guidelines for improvement. The individual concerned should have had an opportunity to explain what happened before a decision to dismiss is made, and have the right to be represented by a shop steward or colleague.

If the tribunal does find a dismissal unfair they may make a re-instatement order (giving the same job back) or a re-engagement order (similar job) if the applicant wishes this. A compensatory award may also be made.

8.7 Health and safety at work

Throughout the chapter we have been looking at the relationship between the employer and the employee and the laws that support this. The final area to consider is the employer's and employee's duty for health and safety at work.

The main law in this area is the Health and Safety at Work Act 1974 which gives a duty of care to all employers to ensure, so far as is reasonably practicable, the health and safety of all who may be affected by what the organisation does or fails to do. The Health and Safety at Work Act 1974 provides a framework piece of legislation under which specific regulations and codes of practice can be drafted, amended or withdrawn as appropriate. The act also introduced some specific duties for employers including:

❑ the requirement to ensure that all working practices are safe;

❑ the work environment must be safe and healthy;

❑ all plant and equipment must be provided and kept up to the necessary standard;

In addition, information, training and supervision should be provided and the company's safety policy communicated to all employees. Safety representatives and safety committees should be set up to monitor safety measures and assist the employer in providing effective work systems.

The employee also has a duty:

☐ to take reasonable care of him/herself and others;

☐ to allow the employer to carry out his duties;

☐ not to interfere intentionally or recklessly with any machinery or equipment.

As well as the Health and Safety at Work Act 1974 there are specific laws applying to certain premises. The main ones are the Factories Act 1961 and the Offices, Shops and Railway Premises Act 1963. E.U. law is also a significant factor, particularly the 6 directives that were adopted by the U.K. on the 1st January 1993. These directives are:

1. a general framework directive adding the following general duties for employers:

    ☐ they must carry out continuous risk assessment, generally in writing, of all work hazards;

    ☐ they must introduce controls to reduce risks;

    ☐ they must share hazard and risk information with other employers, including those on adjoining premises, other site occupiers and all subcontractors coming on to the premises;

    ☐ they should revise safety policies in the light of the above, or initiate safety policies if none were in place previously;

    ☐ they must identify employees who are especially at risk;

    ☐ they must provide fresh and appropriate training in safety matters;

    ☐ they must provide information to employees (including temps) about health and safety;

    ☐ they must employ competent health and safety advisors.

Employees also have an additional duty to inform their employer of any situation which may be a danger or risk to health and safety.

2. health and safety requirements for the workplace;

3. safety and health requirements for the use of work equipment at work;

4. the use of personal protective equipment;

5. the manual handling of loads where there is a risk, particularly of back injury to workers;

6. health and safety requirements for work with display screen equipment.

Managing health and safety can be divided into the following areas:

☐ safe systems of work;

☐ general working environment;

☐ accidents and emergencies;

☐ health problems.

Safe systems of work require all potential hazards to be identified in the workplace.

Activity

List as many possible hazards as you can in the workplace, and consider how risks from these can be reduced.

There are many hazards but these are some of the main areas:

☐ use of machinery, plant and equipment;

☐ chemicals and toxic substances (radiation, gas and dust etc);

☐ fire and explosion;

☐ noise and vibration;

☐ heat/cold;

☐ stress/fatigue;

☐ transport and handling materials (stacking and lifting);

☐ falls (working at a height).

For all hazards careful measurement must take place to determine the safe exposure level or work system required. These are often covered by the Codes of Practice and regulations mentioned before. For hazardous activities a permit to work system should be introduced so only qualified and trained personnel are used. Protective equipment should be provided where necessary and work systems designed to minimise hazards in the first place. All employees should be trained in safe working practices, and supervised effectively. Adequate breaks and rest periods must be allowed to ensure there is no undue fatigue (a common cause of accidents). Plant and materials must be regularly maintained and inspected. Safety representatives and safety committees should constantly review provision to ensure it is adequate and all hazards have been identified.

General working environment – As well as the risks identified above the general working environment should be monitored to ensure there is:

☐ adequate hygiene and welfare;

☐ work areas are ergonomically designed with correct seating and desk levels;

☐ temperature and humidity is controlled;

☐ lighting is adequate;

☐ there is no excessive noise.

Accidents and emergencies – In the event of an accident or emergency taking place the following items are recommended by the Health and Safety Executive:

Tell people: ☐ what might happen and how the alarm will be raised;

☐ what to do, including how to call the emergency services;

☐ where to go to reach safety or get rescue equipment;

☐ who will control the incident, and the names of other key people such as the first aiders;

□ essential actions such as emergency plant shut down or making processes safe.

Checklist: □ keep any access ways for emergency services and all escape routes clear;

□ clearly label important items like shut off valves, electrical isolators and fire fighting equipment;

□ make sure emergency plans cover night and shift working, weekends and (possibly) times when the premises are closed eg holidays;

□ train everyone in emergency procedures, eg fire drills, and don't forget the special needs of disabled people;

□ test emergency equipment regularly – disposable eyewash bottles should not have been opened and used, for example;

□ assist the emergency services by clearly marking your premises from the road. Consider drawing up a simple plan marked with the location of hazardous items;

□ have a system to account for staff and visitors in the event of evacuation.

Activity

Consider what measures are necessary when planning how to respond to a fire at the work premises.

All employees should be aware of the sound of a fire bell and the emergency evacuation process that should follow. Exits should be clearly marked, customers helped to leave the premises if applicable, and all toilets or store rooms checked. Lifts should not be used. Fire extinguishers should be clearly marked as to type and use, and fire officers should be instructed in their operation. After evacuation all staff should be accounted for and nobody should re-enter the premises until told that it is safe by a fire officer.

First aid treatment and an adequate number of staff qualified in first aid should be organised by the management. All injuries should be recorded in the accident book, some must be reported immediately to the Health and Safety inspectors where someone dies, receives a major injury, or is seriously affected by, for example, electric shock or poisoning, and if there is a dangerous occurrence (near miss).

Health problems – Employers have a duty to decide if an employee is fit to work. Some jobs require particular physical requirements and the individuals performing them must be constantly monitored to ensure they are not at risk. Illness or injury may affect any employee's ability to perform their job so those returning to work after illness or injury may need time to re-adjust to their tasks.

The use of drugs (prescribed or illegal) or alcohol may significantly affect the employee's competence and safety. Counselling/discipline is needed to deal with people affected in this way.

Work related illnesses or injuries are particularly serious. Work related upper limb disorders have been linked to V.D.U. usage or repetitive movements. The E.U. directive mentioned before should be implemented in full. Individuals experiencing health problems must be encouraged to visit their G.P. or doctors/nurses from the Employment Medical Advisory Service for a medical examination.

8.8 Summary

In this chapter the essential elements of employee relations have been covered from both a collective and individual viewpoint. The chapter began by examining current trends in trade union membership and the role and function of unions today. The processes of negotiation and collective bargaining were outlined and the sanctions that could be used by both parties to advance their case were reviewed. Conflict resolution mechanisms of conciliation, mediation and arbitration were also covered. The processes of communication, consultation and participation were described to show other methods of collective involvement within an organisation. A summary of current labour law was included to give an overview of its role in regulating employment. The importance of company rules and effective grievance and disciplinary procedures was emphasised and the law in the area of dismissal outlined. The chapter ended with a review of Health and Safety, incorporating a discussion of the management processes involved in designing and implementing safe systems of work and a healthy environment.

Further reading

ACAS Advisory Handbook: *Discipline at Work*

Brewster C, *Employee Relations*, 1989, Macmillan Education Ltd

Farnham D & Pimlott J, *Understanding Industrial Relations* (4th edition) 1990, Cassell Educational Ltd

Fowler A, *Negotiation skills and strategies*, IPD

Green G D, *Industrial Relations Text and Case Studies* (4th edition) 1994, Pitman Publishing

Greenhalgh R, *Industrial Tribunals*, IPD Law and Employment Series

Health and Safety Executive: *Essentials of Health and Safety at Work*

Lewis D, *Essentials of Employment Law*, IPD

Pope C, *Working with the Unions*, IPD Law and Employment Series

Salamon M, *Industrial Relations Theory and Practice*, 1989, Prentice Hall

Suter E, *The Employment Law Checklist* (5th edition), IPD

Exercises

Progress questions

These questions have been designed to help you remember the key points in this chapter. The answers to the questions are on p127

Complete the following sentences:

1. The Trade Union Congress is...

2. The outcomes of collective bargaining are either...or

   .... agreements.

3. Mediation is a process where..

4. The function and purpose of an Industrial Tribunal is...

5. The main legislation in the area of Health and Safety is..

Select the correct response to the following statements:

6. The Transport and General Worker's Union is the largest trade union in the U.K.

   True ☐ False ☐

7. If a trade union can demonstrate that a majority of employees are members of the union, the employer must recognise that union for negotiation and collective bargaining.

   True ☐ False ☐

8. It is illegal for an employer to discriminate against a job applicant because they are a member of a trade union.

   True ☐ False ☐

9. The right not to be unfairly dismissed was included in the Employment Protection (Consolidation) Act 1978.

   True ☐ False ☐

10. Conciliation is where a third party makes a binding decision based on proposals made by both parties in a dispute.

    True ☐ False ☐

Review questions

These questions have been designed to help you check your comprehension of the key points in this chapter. You may also wish to look further than the text in this chapter in order to answer them fully. You will find your library useful as a source of wider reading. You can check the essential elements of your answers by referring to the appropriate section.

11. Outline the main factors that have caused trade union membership to decline in the 1980's and 90's. (Section 8.2)

12. Detail the main stages through which a negotiation will pass before reaching agreement. (Section 8.3)

13. Explain the difference between communication, consultation and participation giving examples of each. (Section 8.4)

14. Explain how the law on immunity from prosecution is applied to both individuals and trade unions in dispute with an employer. (Section 8.5)

15. List the 5 main areas that provide a fair reason for dismissal giving examples of each. (Section 8.6)

16. What are the main stages that need to be addressed when planning safe systems of work. (Section 8.7)

Multiple choice questions

The answers to these questions are given in the Lecturer's Supplement.

17. With which of the following bodies do trade unions need to register to be legal?
    a) the Commissioner for the Rights of Trade Union Members
    b) the Trade Union Congress
    c) the Arbitration, Conciliation, and Advisory Service
    d) the Certification Officer

18. The total number of registered trade unions in 1994 was:
    a) 452
    b) 1,300
    c) 267
    d) 148

19. A newly appointed employee has the following right to maternity leave:
    a) None
    b) 14 weeks
    c) 29 weeks
    d) 52 weeks

Practice questions

A marking guide to these questions is given in the Lecturer's Supplement.

20. Review the effectiveness of picketing as a trade union sanction and outline the main features of the code of practice on picketing.

21. Outline the basic rights of employees who are made redundant under the Employment Protection (Consolidation) Act 1978.

22. Detail what is needed to ensure a disciplinary procedure works effectively.

Questions for advanced students

> *A marking guide to these questions is given in the Lecturer's Supplement.*

23. How effective do you think current employment law is in regulating the relationship between employers and employees?

24. How much power do you feel the largest union UNISON has in negotiation and collective bargaining in the public sector?

Assignment: Shop steward concerns at Freshfield's NHS Trust

A marking guide to this assignment is given in the Lecturer's Supplement.

Freshfield's N.H.S. Trust recognises the UNISON trade union for collective bargaining and has a full programme of health and safety assessment, safety representatives and safety committees. You are the Human Resource Manager for the Trust.

You received a visit yesterday from Rodney Thomas the UNISON shop steward who is also a member of the safety committee. He brought the following matters to your attention and is returning to see you today to hear your response. The issues he raised were:

i)   Staff cutbacks in the number of hospital porters has meant that there are fewer staff available for lifting and transporting patients. Other auxiliary staff, not trained in manual handling and lifting, are helping out and Rodney believes they should not be undertaking this work. He wants to hear what action you will take regarding this problem.

ii) Daphne McPherson, a black student nurse, has told Rodney that she is being harassed and is receiving racist verbal abuse from two other trainees at the hospital. Rodney would like to discuss how you intend to handle this issue within the established grievance and disciplinary procedures.

Required

Prepare some written notes on both issues to assist you in your forthcoming meeting with Rodney.

Appendix

Answers to Progress questions

Chapter 1

1. The welfare tradition is based on the belief that employees are more motivated and work more efficiently if good standards of welfare, health and safety are provided by the employer.

2. Scientific management was the term used to describe the breaking down and analysing of jobs in order to find the best way to organise tasks to increase productivity and work efficiency.

3. Industrial relations is primarily concerned with the collective relationships between employers and employees.

4. Characteristics of the personnel management approach include a specialist role for the function with an advisory and administrative focus, an emphasis on written rules and procedures, tightly defined jobs with collective rewards and benefits, a command and control management hierarchy and a conflict generating system of collective bargaining and negotiation.

5. Characteristics of HRM include a central, strategic role for the function, with more emphasis on the contributions of line managers, flexible and loosely defined jobs, a team based management approach, individual rewards and benefits and conflict minimised by consultation and participation.

6. False

7. True

8. True

9. False

10. False

Chapter 2

1. The mission statements of the organisation are statements that set out the future objectives and key tasks of the organisation or work group.

2. Work teams can be created around a variety of groupings including functions, geographical areas, products, time periods (shifts), customer bases or forms of technology.

3. Task flexibility is where work is organised flexibly so that a wide range of tasks are identified for jobs at each level rather than jobs consisting of a narrow set of rigidly defined and restricted tasks.

4. The management control systems of an organisation aim to organise work flow and productivity by determining the standards required and then monitoring to ensure these standards are being met taking corrective action where necessary.

5. The 3 skill sets needed by a manager are human (interpersonal) skills, technical (decision/knowledge) skills and conceptual (planning/visionary) skills.

124

6. True
7. False
8. True
9. False
10. False

Chapter 3

1. Human resource planning is about preparing to meet the present and future needs of the organisation by determining the numbers and skills required of employees.

2. Trend analysis assists demand forecasting by analysing historical data to help identify trends which can then be projected forward to help predict demand in the future.

3. The most significant demographic trends affecting the U.K. workforce are the fall in the number of young people joining the workforce, and the resulting increase in numbers of older workers, also the greater numbers of women joining the workforce accompanied by an increase in part-time employment.

4. Job design involves establishing the relationships that should exist between the job holder and other members of the department or section, deciding on the content of a job in terms of its duties and responsibilities and determining the methods to be used in carrying out the job.

5. A job description would be called generic if it covers not just a single job but a set of related jobs (job families).

6. False
7. True
8. True
9. False
10. False

Chapter 4

1. A person specification is a description of the qualities and skills that must be possessed by an individual in order to be able to perform the job.

2. The 3 most important details looked for in a job advertisement are the job title, location and salary.

3. Bias in interviewing can be minimised by the comparison of all candidates with objectively set criteria established before the interview begins, the use of more than one interviewer, and training of interviewers to help them recognise where bias may occur.

4. Special aptitude tests are measures of one type of ability or job aptitude such as verbal ability, computer aptitude etc

5. The validity of a selection technique is a measure of how well the results gained from the exercise matched with the actual ability of the individual to perform the task or job.

6. True
7. True
8. False

9. False

10. False

Chapter 5

1. Direct discrimination is where individuals are treated less favourably on the grounds of their sex, marital status or race.

2. Genuine occupational qualifications are requirements of the job that mean that only people of one sex or race can fulfil them.

3. The main Act covering racial discrimination is the Race Relations Act 1976.

4. Positive action programmes are designed to target applicants from under-represented groups in the workforce and encourage them to apply for suitable vacancies.

5. The main ethnic grouping to be included on a monitoring forms are African, Asian, Caribbean, U.K. European, Chinese, Cypriot, Irish, Other European, Any other (please specify).

6. False

7. False

8. True

9. False

10. False

Chapter 6

1. Experiential learning can be analysed into 4 stages, these are feeling (experiencing), observing (reflection), thinking through the implications (forming abstract concepts and generalisations) and experimenting (applying principles).

2. NVQ's are divided into units which are then subdivided into elements, performance criteria and range statements.

3. Comparative appraisal is a method which assesses an employees performance relative to other members of his/her work group or department.

4. A training need arises when the knowledge, skill or behaviour demanded exceeds current capabilities.

5. The most common methods used to convey knowledge are lectures, handouts, books and manuals.

6. True (but GNVQ's are available to those in full-time education)

7. True

8. True

9. False

10. True

Chapter 7

1. The five characteristics of good objectives summed up in the acronym S.M.A.R.T. are that they should be specific, measurable, agreed, reasonable and time bound.

2. Job classification is a method of job evaluation which defines the number of grades in the pay structure and then provides a description of the characteristics of the jobs found in each grade.

3. The term harmonisation means bringing all systems of pay and remuneration within the organisation on to the same basis.

4. A pay spine is a system of increments using continuous, non-overlapping, pay scales.

5. Profit sharing payment schemes are schemes that pay a bonus to employees which is related in some way to the profits earned by the business.

6. False

7. True

8. False

9. True

10. True

Chapter 8

1. The Trade Union Congress is a collective body which provides a voice for the trade union movement, regulates union behaviour, conducts research and generally promotes trade unionism.

2. The outcomes of collective bargaining are either substantive or procedural agreements.

3. Mediation is a process where a third party (often ACAS) proposes recommendations for both parties in dispute to consider.

4. The function and purpose of an Industrial Tribunal is to resolve cases brought under the various employment laws speedily and informally.

5. The main legislation in the area of health and safety is the Health and Safety at Work Act 1974.

6. False (UNISON is the largest union)

7. False

8. True

9. True

10. False

Index

Essential Elements

covering the core for **modular** courses

Essential Elements of **Management Accounting** *Jill & Roger Hussey*

Contents The role of management accounting; Cost classification and control; Total costing; Marginal costing; Capital investment and appraisal; Budgetary control; Standard costing; Appendices.   **ISBN** 1 85805 103 7

Essential Elements of **Financial Accounting** *Jill & Roger Hussey*

Contents The accounting framework; Users and uses of financial information; The cash flow forecast; The profit and loss account for a sole trader; The balance sheet for a sole trader; The financial statements of a limited company; Interpretation of financial statements.   **ISBN** 1 85805 091 X

Essential Elements of **Business Economics** *Mark Sutcliffe*

Contents: The UK economy – an overview; Resource allocation; Business costs; The structure of business and its conduct; Small firms and multinationals; Wages and the labour market; Investment, R & D and training; National economic change and business activity; Money, banking and inflation; Economic policy and the business environment; The international dimension; Europe and business.   **ISBN** 1 85805 095 2

Essential Elements of **Business Statistics** *Les Oakshott*

Contents Survey Methods, Presentation of data, Summarising data, Probability and decision making, The Normal Distribution, Analysis and interpretation of sample data, Testing a hypothesis, Correlation and regression.   **ISBN** 1 85805 103 7

Essential Elements of **Quantitative Methods** *Les Oakshott*

Contents: Index numbers, Investment appraisal, Time series analysis, Linear programming, Critical path analysis, Stock control methods, Simulation.   **ISBN** 1 85805 098 7

Essential Elements of **Business Information Systems** *Brian Corr*

Contents: Information; Systems theory; Management; Decision making; Developing information systems; Databases and DBMS; Modelling.   **ISBN** 1 85805 136 3

Essential Elements of **Marketing** *R Smith*

Contents: What is marketing?; The product; Promotion; Selling as part of marketing; Pricing policy; Place and distribution; Marketing research; Marketing management   **ISBN** 1 85805 102 9

All titles in this series are approximately 128 pages long, and measure 275 x 215mm.

Tackling Coursework

Projects, Assignments, Reports and Presentations

David Parker

This book provides the student with practical guidance on how to approach the coursework requirement of a typical business studies course, i.e. projects, assignments, reports and presentations. The text makes clear the different approaches needed for the different types of coursework, with examples of each in an Appendix, and there is advice on how to conduct research, collect information and present results, in either written or verbal form. It is expected to be used on the following courses: any business studies course at undergraduate (e.g. BABS) or postgraduate (e.g. MBA) level. It would also be useful as a preparatory text for a research degree.

Contents:

Introduction, Dissertations and projects, Essays and papers, Management reports, Seminars and presentations, Research methods. **Appendices:** *Further reading, Example of a dissertation proposal, Example of citations, Dissertation contents, Example of an essay.*

1st edition • 96 pp • 215 x 135 mm • 1994 • ISBN 1 85805 101 0